Did you put your name and address on the lines above? Then you failed, and you need this book more than you know. Con artists often need to vanish in a hurry, from a card game, bar, hotel lobby, you name it. They never leave proof behind—business cards, name tags, credit card receipts—that they were ever there.

Just one of countless con tips you'll find in this book. And from now on, if somebody asks you to write your name in a book—don't.

THE MODERN CON MAN

How to Get Something for Nothing

Todd Robbins
& the Modern Conman Collective

Gadi Harel
Marcel Sarmiento
Jack Silbert

Illustrations by Mike Phi

BLOOMSBURY

Published by Bloomsbury USA, New York
Distributed to the trade by Macmillan

All papers used by Bloomsbury USA are natural, recyclable products made from
wood grown in well-managed forests. The manufacturing processes conform to the
environmental regulations of the country of origin.

LIBRARY OF CONGRESS CATALOGING-IN-PUBLICATION
DATA HAS BEEN APPLIED FOR.

ISBN-10: 1-59691-453-x
ISBN-13: 978-1-59691-453-7

First U.S. Edition 2008

1 3 5 7 9 10 8 6 4 2

Designed and typeset by Hollywoodmade
Printed and bound in Singapore by Tien Wah Press Ltd

To the suckers, without whom none of this would be possible.

CONTENTS

Introduction • *"The Roper"*   ix

Chapter 1 • **BAR BETS**   1
How to Scam Your Way to a Free Beer

Chapter 2 • **WORK WAGERS**   33
How to Con Your Coworkers

Chapter 3 • **"FRIENDLY" WAGERS**   61
Bets with Buddies and Fooling Your Friends

Chapter 4 • **CARD CONS**   87
Poker Night Games and Other Ways to Con a Card Player

Chapter 5 • **CONTINENTAL GRIFT**   115
"Con the Road Again . . ."

Chapter 6 • **SCAMS IN LOVE**   143
Cupid Cons and Other Ways to Avoid a Valentine's Day Massacre

Chapter 7 • **SPORT SCAMS**   171
Ways to Grift at Game Time

Chapter 8 • **COLLEGE CONS**   197
Ways to Scam at School

In Conclusion • *"Blow Off"*   225

Acknowledgments   226

INTRODUCTION
"THE ROPER"

Do unto others . . . then run.

This is my motto. It will become the motto of those who read and embrace the philosophy put forth in these pages. There is nothing nice about this book. You see, it all boils down to one simple fact: The world is rapidly becoming separated into the Deceivers and the Deceived. The sooner you decide which group you want to be in, the better off you will be.

And there is no shame in wanting to be one of the Deceived. In stupidity there is bliss. So head over to the next aisle and pick up some self-help book featured on *Oprah*. This book was not written for you. You are a nice person. You believe we should do unto others as we would have done to us. And if it were not for sweet people like you, the people for whom this book is written would have no one to scam.

If you are like me (and I know I am), you would rather be predator than prey. If this is the case, then boy oh boy, this book was written for you, my friend. So enjoy.

—Todd Robbins

PS: And if you bought this book online or from some other source and you didn't know what you were getting, then e-mail me at coneyislandtodd@aol.com and I will refund the money you spent on the book. Just include the name of your bank and your account number, and I will send the money directly to your bank. And so that there are no mix-ups, include your social security number and your mother's maiden name. Thanks, I'll take it from there.

CHAPTER 1

BAR BETS

How to Scam Your Way to a Free Beer

Late at night in a dark bar, loud music thumping, alcohol flowing, people pushing through a crowd: This is the perfect playground for an experienced con artist. Distractions abound. And did we mention the alcohol? Impaired judgment can make for a very easy mark. You may never have to pay for a beer again.

But before you read on, there's one crucial caveat: An angry drunk doesn't appreciate being scammed. So always case out the exit.

THE
BLOW
HOLE

One of the smartest wagers you can make is betting people who've been drinking that they can't do even the simplest of tasks. That's what makes this so incredibly easy . . . you don't have to do anything. It's all on them.

WHAT IT'S GOOD FOR:
Flirting. And flirting your way to a free drink.

WHAT YOU NEED:
- An empty beer bottle
- A cocktail napkin

WHAT YOU DO:

1 Rip off a piece of the cocktail napkin and roll it into a tiny raisin-size ball.

2 Hold the empty beer bottle perfectly horizontal. No tilting at all.

3 Place the napkin ball just inside the lip of the bottle's opening.

4 Challenge your mark to blow the napkin ball into the bottle (see fig. 1).

WHAT'S THE SECRET:

Couldn't sound easier, right? Actually, it's impossible.* Because, as simple as it sounds, it can't be done. You will never lose. Huff and puff and blow the house down, that napkin ball ain't going in. It's some sort of physics thing: Your breath goes in, bounces off the back, and blows the ball back out at you. If your mark wants to try again, say yes, and quickly figure out which drink you're betting for. (Also works with a cigarette butt, in which case it's pleasantly named "Butt in Your Face.")

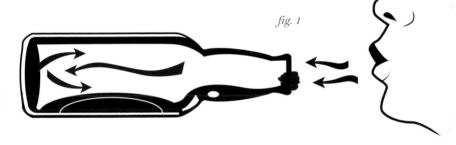

fig. 1

---

* And yet, if the tables are turned and *you've* been told to do it, there *is* a cheap way. You agree to try on the condition that if you can do it, they buy your drinks for the rest of the night. You blow on the ball . . . with a straw. The concentrated stream of air will cause the ball to roll right into the bottle.

I first learned this one many years ago in Eddie Farquar's bar in Split Lip, North Dakota, where I was stuck due to a blizzard. It turns out the bartender, Eddie himself, and I both learned a thing or two from the legendary grifter Ol' Doc Shannon. But that afternoon, Eddie taught me the BLOW HOLE, so I decided to kill some time by having fun with the locals. I won so many free drinks, I only sobered up last Tuesday. Thanks, Eddie. —TR

ICEBREAKERS

Before working your marks, a little conversation to relax and distract them isn't a bad idea. Here are thirteen bar-friendly factoids to help you on your way . . .

1

The pressure in a bottle of champagne
is about 90 pounds per square inch.

2

The average number of grapes it takes
to make a bottle of wine is six hundred.

3

A labeorphilist is a collector of beer bottles.

4

Cenosillicaphobia is the fear of an empty glass.

5

If you put a raisin in a glass of champagne,
it will repeatedly float to the top and sink to the bottom.*

6

The bubbles in Guinness beer sink to the bottom
rather than float to the top as in other beers.**

---

* The raisin will sink at first for the same reason other things do: It is more dense than the drink. What happens here, though, is that the raisin's texture catches some of the bubbly's rising gas bubbles. By the time the raisin reaches the bottom, the collected bubbles are collectively strong enough to bring it back to the surface—where the bubbles immediately burst. The raisin then finds itself falling again . . .

** After the drink is poured, the gas bubbles rise from the bottom. However, the bubbles on the side are slowed down as they drag along the surface of the glass, which means the central bubbles shoot up much faster. Hitting the top (or, in fact, the bottom of the head of the beer), these bubbles are pushed

7

There are 293 ways to make change for a dollar.

8

Attila the Hun was suspected of suffocating from a bloody
nose after passing out at his "bachelor party."

9

Prohibition lasted 13 years, 10 months, 19 days,
17 hours, and 32 1/2 minutes.

10

Beer, as with all alcoholic drinks, is made by fermentation:
Bacteria feeds on yeast cells, then defecates.
This bacterial excrement is called alcohol.

11

The most expensive beer, at fifty-two dollars a bottle,
is Tutankhamen, made from a recipe found in
Queen Nefertiti's temple in Egypt.

12

The Whistler Tree in Portugal is the world's
largest cork tree, producing enough cork each
harvest for one hundred thousand wine bottles.

13

Turtles can breathe through their butts.

---

outward, where they again hit a wall—this time the side of the glass—and
are forcibly pushed downward by the strong current of bubbles following
behind. Even though this creates a circular path for the bubbles, all we can
see are the ones coming down the sides. This happens in most drinks where
bubbles rise. But Guinness is dispensed with a mix of nitrogen and carbon
dioxide (as opposed to just carbon dioxide like most beers), and it's the
nitrogen that makes the difference. Its bubbles don't dissolve as easily, and
it's what gives the beer its thick, creamy head and smooth texture. The
combination of dark liquid and light-colored crème bubbles makes the
"sinking" phenomenon more visible than with other beverages.

Enough. Too much thinking, not enough drinking.

NIM *

Supposedly an old Egyptian game—though we're guessing they didn't use matches. You won't lose and it'll drive your victims crazy. You'll win drink after drink after drink, as long as the marks want a rematch.

WHAT IT'S GOOD FOR:
Scam a thinker, someone reading a book, solving a crossword, etc.

WHAT YOU NEED:
• 20 matches (with a 21st at hand just in case)

WHAT YOU DO:

1 Spill twenty matches on the counter and challenge your opponent to a fun little game.

2 Explain the rules: Each player can remove one, two, or three matches during his turn. Whoever is left with the last match loses.

3 Follow the "First Turn Instructions" to make sure your opponent is left with seventeen matches.

4 PAY ATTENTION, THIS IS THE KEY: From this point on, make sure you and your opponent's turns add up to four. So if he takes one, you take three. If he takes three, you take one, and if he takes two, you take two.

5 When your opponent wants to try again, avoid any lame match/rematch jokes.

FIRST TURN INSTRUCTIONS:

- If you go first:
  Pick up three matches, so there are seventeen left in the pile.

- If your opponent goes first and takes one match:
  Take two matches, so there are seventeen left in the pile.

- If your opponent goes first and takes two matches:
  Take one match, so there are seventeen left in the pile. (Noticing a pattern?)

- If your opponent goes first and takes three matches, there are two ways to handle the situation. Keep one extra match under your thigh on the bar stool. Matches are tiny and easy to conceal in your hand. Reach into the pile with the concealed match and "pick" that match. Then there are still seventeen in the pile. If you can't sneak another match in, there's a trickier way to do this. Do your best and try and reach one of these other key numbers after one of your turns—**thirteen**, **nine**, or **five**. If you get to one of them, go back to your trick of adding up to four. As long as your opponent is left with five matches at the end, you can't lose.

---

* The name can mean either "take" or "steal"—which says it all.

This was a favorite game of the infamous gambler Nicholas Andreas Dandolos, also known as Nick the Greek. It has been said he once won two hundred thousand dollars playing this game. Of course, he lost three hundred thousand dollars the next day playing the ponies, but that's beside the point. —TR

"IN-THE-KNOW"
NIM

Grifters have been playing this game for years. And not just with marks, but with each other too. How can that be, you ask? We'll tell you. They take a bunch of matchboxes and dump the contents out on the table. No one knows how many matches are there, so when they start playing, what's really going on is a test to see who can visually count the pile of matches the fastest. Once the number of matches is determined, which can take a few turns before the pile gets down to a countable number, it is a dance of death to get to one of the key numbers. It keeps us grifters on our toes.

THE DILEMMA OF SCRUPLES

I've heard about these things called scruples. I think it's the name of the currency in some Eastern European country or something.

Scruples are needed only if everyone in life is playing fair. They're not. You have no idea just how far the deck is stacked against you.

Every time you meet someone, you have to size him up and see if he is for you or against you. Chances are he is against you. And even the ones that are for you right now can turn on you in a second. So my advice is "screw unto others before they screw unto you."

But if you still feel it best not to deceive your fellow man, all I ask is—*please*—don't dummy up a mark. Never help out some poor soul who is about to be taken by letting him know he is about to be taken.

If you see someone trying to scam someone else (especially if that first guy is the handsome man whose photograph is found on the jacket of this book), just let it happen. Keep your yap shut and walk away. Or stand off to the side, watch the scam play out, and learn something about the way this stuff should work. But don't jump in, explain to the mark what is happening, and try to save the day like some friggin' superhero. The victim will hate you (even more than the scammer will) because to him you have shown how superior and noble you are by thwarting evil. And in doing so, you have made him feel stupid.

So keep your yap shut and walk away.

LAY OF THE LAND

Many wagers from the following chapters can also be modified to work at a bar. But where exactly to spring a scam is almost as important as which scam to spring.

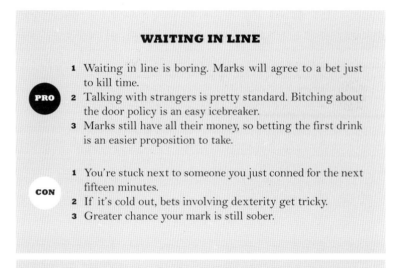

WAITING IN LINE

PRO

1 Waiting in line is boring. Marks will agree to a bet just to kill time.
2 Talking with strangers is pretty standard. Bitching about the door policy is an easy icebreaker.
3 Marks still have all their money, so betting the first drink is an easier proposition to take.

CON

1 You're stuck next to someone you just conned for the next fifteen minutes.
2 If it's cold out, bets involving dexterity get tricky.
3 Greater chance your mark is still sober.

AT THE BAR

PRO

1 Necessary props—shot glasses, olives, mugs, or napkins—are all easily within reach.
2 It's the most acceptable place to talk to a stranger when in a drinking establishment.
3 You're that much closer to your winnings.

CON

1 Potentially little elbow room and counter space.
2 People leaning over to place orders can disrupt your flow.
3 It's more public, and other potential marks can easily see what you're up to.

AT A TABLE OR BOOTH

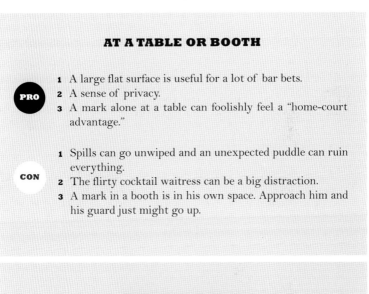

PRO
1 A large flat surface is useful for a lot of bar bets.
2 A sense of privacy.
3 A mark alone at a table can foolishly feel a "home-court advantage."

CON
1 Spills can go unwiped and an unexpected puddle can ruin everything.
2 The flirty cocktail waitress can be a big distraction.
3 A mark in a booth is in his own space. Approach him and his guard just might go up.

IN THE BATHROOM

PRO
1 With a mark out of his comfort zone, it's easier to take control of awkward small talk.
2 The drunker a guy is, the more time he's at the john. And we like drunk marks.
3 When a bar is too noisy, the bathroom can be the quietest place to pull a con.

CON
1 Most likely place to hear "Whoa, dude—you comin' on to me?"
2 Bar staff entering may assume an illegal transaction is taking place.
3 Too many surfaces you'd rather not touch.

THE
WELL-
BALANCED
BET

If there's any bar bet that's hard to pull off after having a few, the WELL-BALANCED BET is it. Which makes it perfect for the mark who's been at the bar a while. Not only will he have trouble guessing the solution, but even after the reveal you can have a laugh watching him fumble an attempt on someone else.

WHAT IT'S GOOD FOR:
Loser pays the "balance" of the winner's tab.

WHAT YOU NEED:
- A shot glass (filled)
- 2 quarters

WHAT YOU DO:
1. Balance the two quarters on the lip of the shot glass (see fig. 1).

2. Challenge your mark to drink the shot without touching the glass with anything other than his lips and mouth or knocking the quarters onto the table or into the drink.

3. When the mark can't, it's your turn. Place the index finger of your dominant hand carefully on one quarter and your thumb carefully on the other. Gently now—don't knock them off. Applying just enough pressure, slide each quarter off the lip of the glass and down to the side.

4. Now you can "grip" the glass as you normally would, but by only touching the quarters (see fig. 2).

5. When you're done with the shot, place the glass back down and slide the quarters up and into the glass. You said the quarters couldn't go into the drink, which they didn't, since there's no more drink left inside. Nor did you ever touch the glass. The quarters were your buffer.

fig. 1

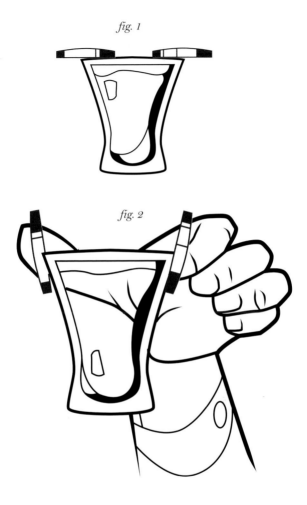

fig. 2

Do this scam early in the evening, before your motor skills have been compromised. This bet, like the HOBOKEN BOTTLE CAP BET (page 16), borders on juggling. So don't just read this and then go out and put it to use. You have to put some practice into it so that it can be done with finesse. Do it smoothly and with a bit of performance. Because if the mark has gotten a bit of a show, he'll be less likely to give you a fast five to the snot box after he has been taken. —TR

DON'T "FREE DRINK" ON AN EMPTY STOMACH

A con man's gotta eat too. So whether you're dishing out cash for overpriced drinks or you've managed to properly scam a few free ones, not having to pay for a meal is a welcome bonus to the evening. Here are a few of our favorite ways to take the edge off, at the right price.

1

Order a dirty martini, extra olives. Health benefits of this mysterious fruit aside, you'll wind up with three or four juicy olives on a little plastic spear. Gulp them down (careful, the spear can be sharp), then order another. Insider tip: Always ask for the extra olives *on the side*. That way you get about a shot more liquor that would otherwise be displaced. And since a martini can be served with cocktail (small pearl) onions instead of olives, you can also ask for "olives and onions on the side"—which gives you more options as well as more drink.

2

There are a wide variety of cocktails that come with other pieces of fruit, like slices of orange and maraschino cherries. Sit close to the bar and you might even be able to snag a few extra pieces on the sly. And if you're open to it, the Bloody Mary can be the holy grail of "fully loaded" drinks. This tomato-and-Tabasco treasure chest is usually garnished with a celery stalk, but can also include a skewer of assorted treats like olives, pickles, carrots, and mushrooms. Some places even slide cheese, salami, and shrimp on those skewers.

3

Bar snacks are not to be overlooked. Whether it's peanuts, pretzels, potato chips, or a heavenly medley of the three, the bottomless bowl of bar snacks is the easiest way to fill up for free. Don't hover or dominate. Play it nice and easy, and the refills will come. Note that some bars, especially those in nice hotels and fancy restaurants, can get creative with their snacks. There's even a place in Los Angeles where you can make a pig of yourself on free bacon.

4

Bar menus and happy hour snacks—while not free—are a smart way to save some dough. If you're meeting for drinks at a restaurant, often the bar area has its own additional menu offering smaller and cheaper options, like one popular steak house chain that offers a plate of four petite filet mignon sandwiches for just three bucks. And like their drink counterparts, happy hour snacks such as wings, mozzarella sticks, and potato skins can sometimes come in two-for-one, half-price, and even, on occasion, unlimited amounts. A word to the wise, though: Go easy on the jalapeño poppers if you want to be at the top of your game.

THE
HOBOKEN
BOTTLE CAP
BET

This one takes practice, but if you get the hang of it, it's a nice little challenge that can impress the opposite sex. As it works best with fancy glassware, such as wine glasses or brandy snifters—and is harder with beer mugs—this is perfect for upscale settings like wine bars and hotel lounges.

WHAT IT'S GOOD FOR:
Seeing who's going to spring for the bottle of 1787 Château Lafite.

WHAT YOU NEED:
- An empty brandy snifter or a red wine glass
- An ashtray or shallow glass
- A bottle cap or olive, cork, etc.

WHAT YOU DO:

1   Challenge your mark to see who can get the bottle cap into the ashtray—but only by using the brandy snifter. Let the mark go first. The person will almost certainly fail, probably trying to flip the cap with the glass's stem or scoop it up into the glass.

2   Now it's your turn. Place the snifter upside down over the bottle cap.

3   Swirl the upside-down glass quickly (see fig. 1), which will—through the magic of science—cause the bottle cap to rise into the glass.

4   Still making the quick swirling motion, lift the glass slowly and move it over the ashtray.

5   Stop swirling the glass. The bottle cap will drop into the ashtray. You win.

fig. 1

The sweet thing about this bit of conology is that you'll be able to sleep the sleep of the innocent, knowing that you won that drink with an honest demonstration of skill. Self-delusion is a wonderful thing. By the way, don't ever try this scam anywhere in Hoboken. There's a story there that I shan't go into at this time, thank you. —TR

Old guy at the end of a bar. The sort of old guy who is always at the end of a bar. As the evening wears on, he leans over toward the twentysomething guy next to him. "I bet you twenty dollars that I can bite my eye," says the old man. The younger guy, a bit buzzed, is clearly amused and agrees to the bet. Without missing a beat, the old man removes his glass eye, puts it in his mouth, and bites it. The young man, realizing he's been had, hands over the twenty and returns to talking to his friends on his other side.

More time passes, and everyone's a little more drunk. The old man taps the young guy's shoulder and regains his attention. "I bet you twenty dollars that I can bite my other eye," he says. The young guy sizes him up and figures he can't pull the same trick—he's not blind, so he can't have two glass eyes. So he takes this bet too. Without missing a beat, the old man removes his false teeth, holds them up to his other eye, and "bites" it. Clearly defeated, the young guy hands over another twenty. He is out forty bucks but has gained a story he can tell the rest of his life.

And who knows, if he ends up as an old guy with a glass eye and false teeth . . .

And if a man bets you he can do something else to himself, just walk away. —*TR*

WHO'S THE MARK?

Every watering hole attracts its own unique mark. So it's wise to wise up on who you might be dealing with.

THE DIVE • The inebriation of your mark is your advantage here, since Lunchtime Lou has been sitting at the bar since noon. Make sure to check his mood, though: If he's singing along to the Eagles on the jukebox and hugging strangers, feel free to use an icebreaker. If he's staring into the mirror behind the bar, wondering how he got to be so old and alone, you might want to explore some other options. While this mark is more like a question mark, if you do find him on the right day, he'll be buying you drinks as you pull one scam after the next, and before you know it, you might even make a brand-new friend.

THE WINE BAR • Since the proposition bet is more common in places like a dive, pulling one in a wine bar has a unique advantage. Snooty Rudy will not only be amused and curious about your unexpected wager, his general sense of superiority will undermine any chance he has. Scams like NIM (math-based and therefore "intellectual") are perfect, since he seems to work mention of his "Harvard years" into every conversation. He will try to turn his eventual loss into some sort of highbrow victory by summing up the experience with a quote by Sartre, such as "Once you hear the details of victory, it is hard to distinguish it from a defeat." Let him. Just get your free drink and walk away, quoting Sartre right back at him: "Hell is other people."

THE DANCE CLUB • Here's where you find Armani Johnny, the mark with too much money and not a care in the world. This could work to your advantage. After all, if you want to bet someone a bottle of champagne, this guy's your man. That is, if he can hear your proposition over the DJ's musical assault.

THE HOTEL BAR • Frequent-Flyer Freddy—he's the one in the rumpled suit and loosened tie who keeps looking around the bar—is just happy to have someone to talk to. Especially since every woman in the place just turned him down. In addition, like the other business types, he's not only bored and looking for entertainment, he's got an expense account. And if that isn't bonus enough, at hotel bars you also have diminished chances of bumping into the same mark twice.

THE SPORTS BAR • Gambling is in the air, and Touchdown Tony is feeling it. Sports bars definitely draw a competitive crowd, who not only want a chance to win, but want a rematch when they lose. This mark thrives on opportunities like "double or nothing" and wholeheartedly believes in "the comeback"—no matter how far he's down. He loves the classic Cinderella story. He dreams of being the one who no one believed in and who came back from nothing to win it all. *Sucker.* So why wait? Go ahead and gain Tony's confidence by engaging him in conversation about whatever game he's watching.

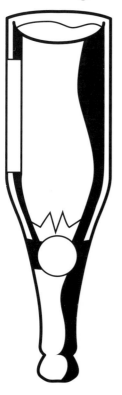

THE
IMPOSSIBLE
DRINK

Bet someone you can drink from the bottle without opening it. Then just flip the bottle over, pour a little of some other drink into the bottom concave part, and "drink from the bottle." Works best with wine and champagne bottles due to their shape. Bet the bartender for the whole bottle of the fancy stuff. If you're going to win a drink, it might as well be top-shelf.

This bit of verbal slipperiness is a favorite of my old friend Mary Piker Douglas. She is a wonderfully innocent-looking lady who could pass for someone's saintly aunt. When she wins the bottle, she has a charming little giggle that makes you want to hug her instead of slug her. —TR

THE
TEN-CENT
SOLUTION

Here's a way to get a glass of wine for as little as a dime. Drop a dime in an empty wine bottle and reseal it with a cork. Then make a bet with the bartender, wagering whether or not another drink is on the house. The challenge: to get the dime without pulling out the cork or smashing the bottle. Sounds impossible. You can shake the bottle, listen to the coin jingle around inside all you want, but that dime doesn't seem like it's going anywhere—unless, that is, you manage to push the cork *in*. Takes some effort, but do that and the dime will slide right into your hand. So will the next drink.

I rarely practice this one. The reason is because pushing that damn cork in the bottle can take effort, and I didn't get into this field of endeavor because I like to break a sweat. Still, this bit will appeal to some scamsters. Many of you pay serious coin so that you can lift heavy things at a gym. Here's another use for all those overdeveloped muscles of yours.
—TR

OUT OF ROOM

For this one you just need a square cocktail napkin and a bunch of the same coins (a lot of pennies or quarters or Malaysian sen, etc.). Take turns putting the coins down on the napkin, one at a time. They can't overlap or stick out over the napkin's edge. Whoever can't put down a coin without having it stick out from the napkin loses. Go!

The trick is to go first and place your quarter right in the middle.* After that, you just mirror your opponent's moves. If he puts one in the lower right corner, you put one in the opposite corner. If he puts a quarter directly above the middle coin, you put one directly below. If you are matching his moves, then as long as he has space for his, you will have space for yours too. And of course, if he doesn't have space, he loses.

---

* If you get the feeling he's going to insist on going first, then when you're setting up the napkins, say, "And in order to set up the game board, we place one quarter right in the middle. Now we're ready to play. You can go first."

CAN'T STAND WAITING

If you're waiting in a line for the bathroom, here's a way to switch places with the guy in front of you. Tell him that you're going to place him against the wall and bet him that he can't stand on his right foot for five seconds while leaning against the wall. If he can't, you can cut in front of him. Just place him against the wall, but not in the way he was expecting. Place him sideways, with his shoulder and the side of his right foot against the wall. Now say, "Lift your left foot for five seconds." You'll see that he'll be lucky to hold it there for half of that.

There's been a lot of talk here about scamming drinks. But that's just plain irresponsible without a lesson in how to get to the loo a little faster. And I'm nothing if not responsible. So consider this lesson complete. —TR

GLOSSARY
OF GRIFT

Ever find yourself using lingo from your job around the girlfriend or your non-work pals? They always shoot you that look and ask, "What the hell are you talking about?" Every occupation has its own terminology. A secret language, really. Con artistry is no exception. Welcome to the con man code.

BAT AWAY

This is the cue given by carnival bosses to the jointees (see page 29) to stop playing the games honestly and start ringing in the gaffs (see page 29). It is a common practice to play the rigged games so that marks (see page 30) win for the first hour of the carnival. This means that all day long there will be folks walking around the midway carrying stuffed animals, the sight of which will give the impression that the games can actually be won.

BEEF

To complain about losing.

BLOW OFF

To get rid of a mark after the con. This may require squaring his beefs, buying him a drink, or dumping his body in a vacant lot in Weehawken, New Jersey.

BOOSTER

To steal something by grabbing it and running like the wind.

CANNON

A pickpocket.

CHILL

To lose interest in a con.

COLD DECK

A deck with cards in the order you want them. So called because when it is switched in during play, it has a lower temperature than the deck being switched out.

CROSSROADER

A traveling grifter (see page 29). See also Single-O (page 30).

CURDLE

To lose control of the con; when something goes wrong.

CUTTING UP TRACES

To meet up after a job and divide up the take. This phrase is also used to describe a session of telling war stories about cons from days gone by. Occasionally these stories are true.

DIP

To pick a pocket; a desperate move.

G ON THE JOINT

A rigged game. The G stands for *gaff* and a joint is the booth where the "game" is being played. This phrase can also be used to find out what angle is being played when you come upon another con artist working a mark, as in "What's the G on the joint with that guy?"

GAFF

Some sort of gimmick that allows the grifter to win and the mark to lose.

GEETUS

Money. Also *semolians, moolah, cabbage, mazooma,* and *filthy lucre.*

GRIFT

To benefit from and/or obtain goods by use of skill rather than violence.

GRIFTER

One who lives by his wits instead of by force; one who grifts.

HEEL AND TOE

To walk out of a restaurant or bar without paying.

INTOXICOLOGIST

A bartender.

JAM AUCTION

A "product introduction and demonstration" that gets the spectators worked up into a frenzy and results in them buying overpriced crap that they really don't want or need. Working a jam auction requires a mastery of crowd psychology.

JOINTEE

A carnival game operator.

JOY JUICE

Booze.

KENTUCKY LAUGHING WATER

Bourbon.

MARK
The victim, or intended victim. Also an *abner*, *chump*, or *patsy*.

PLAY THE C
To win a mark's confidence, the important first step.

PUT THEM ON THE SEND
To send a mark out for more money after he has already lost a few gaffs.

SCAT
Whiskey.

SINGLE-O
A grifter who works alone.

SKIRT
A woman. Also a *dame*, *broad*, *lace*, *Jezebel*, *frill*, *moll*, *Eve*.

SLOUGH
(Rhymes with "rough.") The universal sign to get out and get out now. If you hear someone say "slough," you quietly and quickly find the nearest exit and use it.

SOFT GAME
A friendly card game where no one is suspecting cheating.

STING
To get the mark's money or goods.

SUBWAY DEALER
A card player who tends to deal from the bottom of a deck. Also a *basement dealer*.

TEAR
To cheat your own partner out of some winnings.

TIP A FEW
To have a few drinks.

UP THE COUNTRY/RIVER
In prison.

WHISTLING THROUGH THE GRAVEYARD

To put up a false front or act.

YEGG

A low-life crook. Someone who would read a book like this.

The gods had condemned Sisyphus to ceaselessly rolling a rock to the top of a mountain, whence the stone would fall back of its own weight. They had thought with some reason that there is no more dreadful punishment than futile and hopeless labor.
—ALBERT CAMUS, *THE MYTH OF SISYPHUS*

The Devil finds work for idle hands.
—PROVERB

CHAPTER 2

WORK WAGERS

How to Con Your Coworkers

When con artists find the perfect sucker, they know they need to act fast. Which is why your nightmare nine-to-fiver is every grifter's dream: dozens of marks with nowhere to run. So stop thinking you're stuck in an office with a bunch of lame coworkers and start realizing that they're the ones who are stuck there with you. Yeah, you may fantasize about hitting the road to get a taste of the sting, but the perfect sucker is often right in the next cubicle.

CEO
SLAVE

Takes a little effort but will be worth the return.

WHAT IT'S GOOD FOR:
Hazing the new guy.

WHAT YOU NEED:
- A computer
- Internet connection

WHAT YOU DO:

1 Go to one of the many Web sites that sell domain names and buy one similar to the name of the company you work for. For instance, if you work at Smith Incorporated, and your company's Web address is www.smith.com, buy www.smithinc.com or www.smithcorp.com or www.smith-usa.com. You get the idea. Buying a Web address costs peanuts these days.

2 Follow the directions for setting up webmail and create an e-mail address that's something like ceo@smithcorp.com. When that's done the hardest part is over. It might cost you a couple of bucks a month, but that's nothing compared to the sheer joy it will bring.

3 Using that e-mail address, contact a new employee who hasn't fully acclimated to your office. Welcome him to Smith Inc. and sound like a CEO. Say you like to think of the company as a big family. And add something about how he should not hesitate to let you know if he needs anything. Keep it brief (CEOs don't have a lot of free time), but be very friendly.

4 Odds are, the new guy will return the e-mail with something about being excited to work at Smith. Typical office stuff. He may even say something like "Likewise, if you need anything, let me know." Maybe, maybe not, but it doesn't matter. You can move ahead either way.

5 Now the fun begins. Wait a few days and write back, again from your fake CEO e-mail address. Ask him to do something small for you. If he does it, ask him to do something else. Your requests can get crazier as long as you always keep it sounding legit. Imagine if the CEO wrote you an e-mail saying that there's a woman in your department who he believes smelled of pot yesterday, and since this violates company drug policy, he'd like her scent monitored. Now suddenly the big cheese is asking you to sniff this woman three times a day for the rest of the week and send a detailed scent report on Friday afternoon to this e-mail address. You'd do it, wouldn't you? Especially if he thanked you for taking care of what is surely an odd request, and for confidentiality on this sensitive matter. See, if you make it sound official, as if the new guy's newness is somehow a plus, and he's just the sort of employee the company needs, then your imagination is your only limit. Sit back and watch the fun.

CEO SLAVE is a good thing to try, and try often. There is always someone new coming into the workplace, and they are always eager puppies that want to please. Keep at least one slave around, for you never know when you are going to need someone to stand on a street corner late at night holding a paper bag waiting for it to be picked up by a 350-pound Neanderthal named Tiny. And for more ideas, see page 50. —TR

THE
CREW

Why would a con artist ever work with a crew when he could keep all the "winnings" for himself? Because the savvy grifter knows that with a few helpers in on some larger cons, the profits can increase exponentially. It might be one mild-mannered accomplice, a team of five, or . . . Ocean's Thirteen. Whatever the case, everyone in on a scam has a very specific role to play.

THE
WALL MAN
This is the lookout. He's either watching for cops or other potential trouble, or eyeing passersby for possible marks.

THE
MECHANIC
This is the person actually performing the con. He's the one holding the cards, flashing the smile, making the promise, etc.

THE
SHILL
This seemingly random person is actually a plant who appears to win easily against the mechanic. He encourages other real marks to play along, believing that they have a chance to win as well.

THE
MARK

THE
STICK
He plays an innocent bystander who happens to side with the mechanic. If needed, he makes it seem like the mark is the one trying to pull a fast one.

THE
STEERER
When a wall man spots a potential mark, this accomplice finds ways to "steer" him to the mechanic. This person is also known as a *roper*.

THE
CHILLER
This person steps in if things get heated or out of hand, to calm the mark and smooth out the escape for the mechanic.

TAKE YOUR GARBAGE TO WORK DAY

Bring in something from home that you were just going to throw away anyway: an empty box of cookies or pizza or donuts (you might even want to leave a half-eaten one inside). Leave the box in your kitchen area at work and e-mail everyone saying something like "free donuts in the kitchen," making sure to CC the boss. Your coworkers will find the box empty, assume they've arrived too late, and shuffle off a little let down. And the boss, who'll never actually get up and go get a donut, will be impressed with your generosity. You've scored points with the big guy (not to mention adding to the daily disappointments of everyone else) for doing nothing but bringing your garbage to work.

IMPORTANT NOTE ABOUT THIS SCAM ON PAGE 55

THE
TWO-SPIN SCAM

Here's a fun bet to make with someone who's got a nice hot mug of coffee on his desk. It's also something you'll probably want to practice first so you're not the one who ends up with hazelnut-scented trousers. And practice is all it takes. This is a scam that isn't even a scam. It's a skill you can easily master.

WHAT IT'S GOOD FOR:
Getting a coworker to switch his superior parking space with yours for an entire month.

WHAT YOU NEED:
• A mug of coffee

WHAT YOU DO:

1 Bet the mark that he can't hold the mug and make it spin all the way around twice without letting go of it. Using a mug is best because his natural inclination will be to hold it by the handle, which makes the task virtually impossible.

2 When it's your turn to show him how it's done, take the mug and simply spin in place: Make a 360 with your whole body, twice. The mug will too. This is a cheap victory and your mark will let you know.

3 Now you have him. Make another wager—double or nothing—that you can turn the mug around twice without letting go of it and without moving your feet.

4 The solution is a series of moves that will result in the mug spinning around twice. But the key is to hold the mug from the *bottom* and stay focused on keeping the mug level at all times. Then follow the moves (a, b, c, and d) on the next page.

You can do this with any type of glass, but the mug is best . . . not just because the handle will fool your mark, but because the wide, squat shape makes it easiest to maneuver during the four steps.

I ask you, how can the mark be pissed at losing when you have beaten him with maneuvers that border on interpretive dance? It's a beautiful thing. —TR

THE BEGGAR

THE HEISMAN

a) **THE BEGGAR**: Hold the mug's bottom tightly in your palm, with your hand in front of you.

b) **THE HEISMAN**: Move your elbow out and the mug in toward your armpit.

c) **THE UNDERARM SNEAK**: Now slide the mug under your armpit while swiveling your wrist around and out.

d) **THE FINAL TWIST**: The trickiest part requires concentration to not tip the mug. Your wrist continues to swivel, practically doing a 360, as you raise your hand higher to keep the mug level. Your final position will have your arm up as if you were holding a tray. Now you can carefully return to the "Beggar" position and repeat for the second rotation. Hell, go for a third.

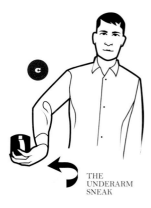

THE
UNDERARM
SNEAK

THE BEGGAR

THE FINAL TWIST

SCREEN SAVIOR

Need a few extra minutes to read a magazine article or talk on the phone? Just go to modernconman.com/screensavior.

You'll find a screen saver that will help it seem as if you're waiting for your computer to do . . . something. If anyone walks by and catches you not working, just shrug toward the screen and say, "The system's so slow today . . ." It can buy you a ten minute time-out whenever you want it.

Ten minutes can save your life (and/or job) if you know what to do with it. —TR

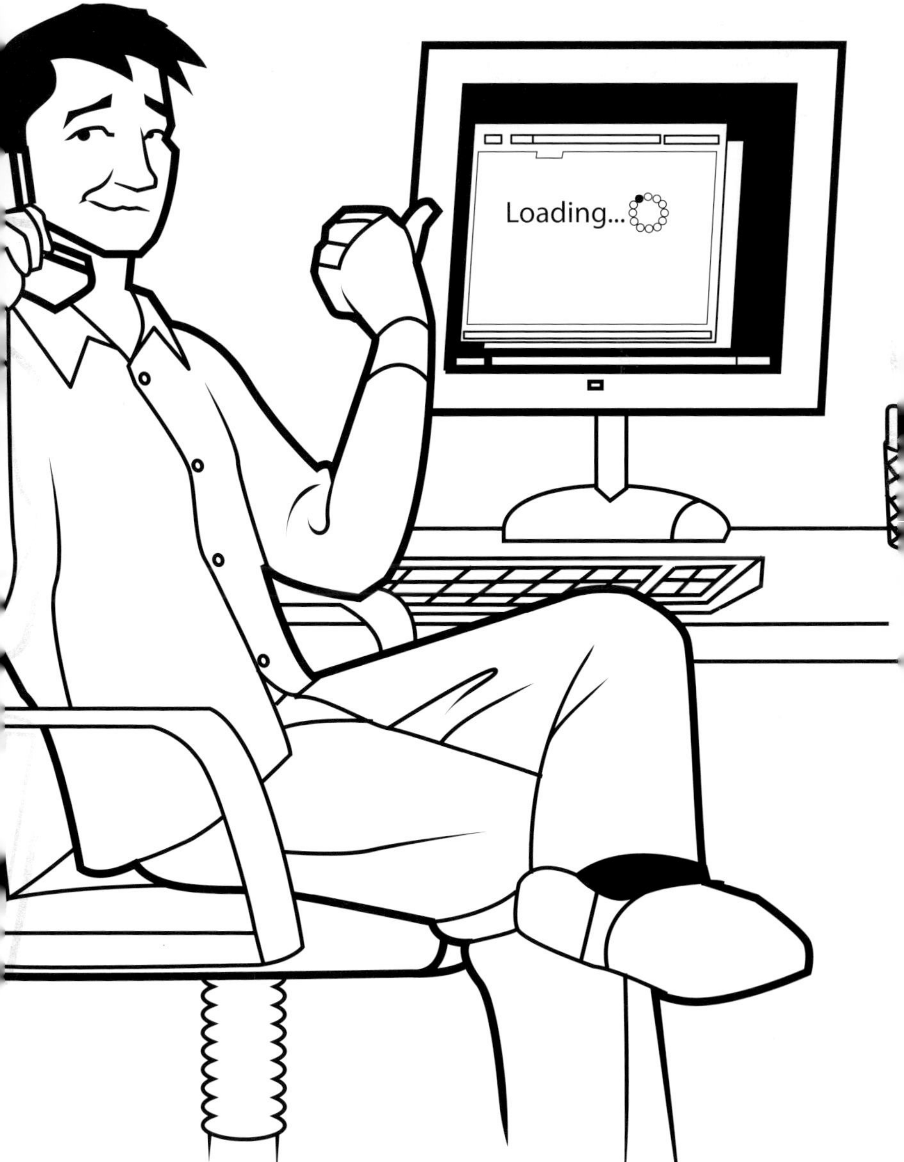
Loading...

CHUMP
CHANGE

Most of the time you can't leave games of chance up to chance, like when you're betting a coworker into picking up the cost of an expensive lunch.

WHAT IT'S GOOD FOR:
Figuring out who's going to pay for the three-martini lunch. Or at least just getting some spare change for the laundry.

WHAT YOU NEED:
- A cup
- 10 coins
- A marker

WHAT YOU DO:

1 Divide the coins equally with the coworker, so you each have five coins.

2 Instruct him to use the marker to write his first initial on each of the coins. When he's done, take the marker and do the same.

3 Drop the ten coins into the cup, swish them around, and dump them back onto the table.

4 Remove the ones that come up initial side down, sliding them off to the side. Take the remaining initial-side-up coins and place them back into the cup.

5 Repeat until one coin remains—the last coin with an initial on it. Whoever's initial it is wins.

WHAT'S THE SECRET:

When it's your turn to write your initial on the coins, make sure to write it on *both* sides of one of them. Since at this point you haven't explained the game, your coworker will not do the same or suspect what you're up to.

This is a lovely, lovely scam. I often keep a two-headed coin on me. There are many uses for a two-headed coin, and this bit of flimflam is one of them. You see, sometimes it will come down to one coin with the mark's initial on it and one with yours. It is conceivable that the mark might notice that your initial jumps from the head of your coin to the tail on the next throw. This would not be a good thing, so that is why I use a two-headed coin.

I would also recommend that you use the neophyte ploy. It is an effective way to get into any scam. You start off by saying, "Hey, let's try something I saw done one time . . ." You then explain and set up the scam with a bit of uncertainty, as if you can't remember exactly how it's done. If you play it just right, your mark's guard will be down and you can just waltz in and pick up your winnings.

It will be an Oscar-worthy performance. No, not that gold statue award thing. I'm talking about Oscar "the Stick" Gonzales, a three-card monte shill down on New York City's Canal Street. —TR

THE **PSYCHIC**
SUCK-UP

There are times, like when you're stuck in the elevator with the boss or, even worse, when he's late and you have to kill time with an important potential client for fifteen minutes, when a little razzle-dazzle can save the day. Besides, we all know that amusing and even impressing the boss is almost as important as taking down your fellow employees.

So let's say you're stuck with a client. Tell him you're getting a good vibe off of him and that you feel he really connects with your company. It's like some sort of mental symbiosis. To prove it, have him write a few numbers on a sheet of paper, shielding it with his hand so you can't see. First, have him write the year he was born and underneath that, a year when something really important happened in his life. Next, he should write the number of years that have passed since that event. Finally, he should write down how old he will be this year. Then tell him to add up all those numbers, again not showing you. Pretend to be "receiving the number" telepathically, and then blurt out the same number he just wrote down. He'll be astounded.

The answer will be two times whatever year this is. The year of birth plus the age will equal this year. And the year of the important event plus the number of years since then will also equal this year. Add 'em up, and you get this year times two.

EMPLOYMENT OPPORTUNITY
FOR THE
MODERN CON MAN

CONS FROM THE JOHN

Taking the skills of the grifter and using them at a "legitimate" job is not out of the question or even out of the ordinary. For more "real world" employment tips for the modern con man, see page 56. Here we learn a little from a former bathroom attendant who worked in many popular New York City strip clubs. As a grifter, he faced one of the most difficult situations imaginable: prying money from men who grip each spare dollar as if it's a potential ticket to paradise.

 How'd you get money from these marks?

I'd make little bets for a buck, like challenging a guy to throw the paper towel into the garbage can. I'd hold the lid open but drop it shut at the last second and the towel would bounce off. Not everyone was amused. But I'd just shrug. The key was just playing it like, "Hey, no biggie. You seemed like the kind of guy who'd get a kick out of that. Forget the buck . . ." and most of them would realize they *wanted* to be the kind of guy who'd get a kick out of that. A dollar went in the jar.

I would also sell them jokes for their next business meeting, or to use on the ladies. And I'd make them laugh—that was key. But most importantly, I would save marriages.

"You going home with that lipstick on your collar?"

"Does your wife have black hair? Because you got a couple of long ones on the back of your shirt."

I always loved that one, because it would work even when there were no hairs. Paranoid married cats would dig deep when I would pull moves like that.

"You're cheaper than a divorce lawyer," they'd tell me after a tip.

LABOR

There is work and then there is *work*. The kind of work that I wish to wax about is not the kind that will provide profit for others and a small bit of reward for you. That kind of labor is known as a *job*.

Those guys in funny white wigs that schemed up these United States put into writing some great ideas you can use to your advantage. One of them is the right to "life, liberty, and the pursuit of happiness." Man, is that a great phrase or what? I'm not talking about the life and liberty part. It is the pursuit of happiness thing that is gold there. Our founding fathers don't promise you happiness, just the chance to chase after it.

Their words imply that happiness is attainable. See, most people live under the impression that if they go to the right school, get the right job (there's that damn word again), and marry the right person, they will find happiness. What the marks fail to grasp is the fact that life is not structured like a paint-by-numbers kit. But believing in the attainability of happiness makes them vulnerable—so let us use this against them, shall we? We will dangle in front of them the mirage that happiness is just beyond their grasp and that if they just do what we ask of them, then they will have that which they desire.

Every grifter of any worth has stumbled onto the fact that life is a never-ending stream of opportunities and challenges. You have to stay alert and play the angles as they come at you if you want to successfully navigate these perilous waters.

So there is work: grinding away doing what others ask of

you and ending up with little to show for your efforts except bitterness and a sense that you have wasted your life. Or there is *work*: dancing along, making the most of all that is swirling about you, building upon your successes so that greater ones will follow, minimizing your failures by learning what you can so you don't repeat them, and ending up with a sense that you have squeezed every ounce of possibility out of life.

If you embrace that latter idea, the results just might be pleasurable. And if you can string together enough pleasure, it comes very close to resembling that mythical beast called happiness.*

---

* Personally, I'm A-OK with pleasure. It's just so much less complicated than happiness. You know it when you have it; there aren't as many existential questions associated with it; losing it is part of the deal, so when it's gone you're not left wondering why; and you always know you'll get it back in one form or another. You can sell happiness to others, but keep the pleasure for yourself.

MORE CEO SLAVE IDEAS

1

"I read a report indicating that warm orange juice increases focus and productivity. Fill the common coffee pot with orange juice."

2

"Check for carpet mites. They are very, very small, so get up close."

3

"My little boy is coming to the office tomorrow. Dress like a clown."

4

"A wrestling team might improve morale. Round up men and women for five different weight classes."

5

" 'My Heart Will Go On' from *Titanic* always lifts my sinking spirits! Once an hour, slowly walk past my office whistling the tune. Don't draw attention to yourself; I'm extremely busy and need to concentrate."

6

"Elevator number three seems a little shaky. Not dangerous, just a little . . . shaky. You can only really feel it if you're sitting on the floor. Try it out for twenty minutes or so."

7

"For a team-building exercise at our off-site, I need you to write an episode of [pick any popular sitcom] but with me as the main character."

8

"Buy a box of paper clips from ten to fifteen local stores, run some tests, and let me know which are the clippiest."

9

"It's [pick a coworker]'s birthday. [Note: It's not really.] Round up some folks and some cake and make it happen."

10

"Find out who the last person to leave the office every night is."

11

"Find out who the earliest person to arrive every morning is."

12

"[Persons A, B, C, and D] are tastemakers. Very casually, play up my intellect, compassion, and physique in conversation with them."

13

"Might be fun to have a chicken in the office. Get us a chicken."

14

"Thinking about a new color scheme. Paint your cubicle green."

15

"Let's have a beach party Friday. Spread some sand around the conference room."

16

"Dress for success. A tuxedo looks sharp. Top hat and tails, my friend!"

17

"I'm worried about people's loyalty. Call a competitor—speak loud enough so others hear—and say you'd like to apply for a job. Track who asks you about it."

18

"At home, I find the windows are cleaner if pretreated with milk. Try it before the cleaning crew comes by."

19

"An official portrait of me would be too pricey with the current budget situation. You seem like a creative type. Do your best."

20

"Homemade egg-salad sandwiches for everyone!"

TIE ONE ON

If at the end of the day you feel like loosening the tie a little, go ahead and just pull the damn thing off. Then take out your frustration with having to wear a tie in the first place by using it to scam a coworker.

WHAT IT'S GOOD FOR:
Deciding which one of you has to wear an excruciatingly awful necktie to work the next day.

WHAT YOU NEED:
• A tie

WHAT YOU DO:
1 Hand the tie to your coworker.
2 Challenge him to hold both ends and—without letting go—tie a knot.
3 After he's unable to, take the tie back and show him how it's done.

WHAT'S THE SECRET:
Instead of just grabbing the left end with your left hand and the right end with your right hand, you have to cross your arms (see fig. 1) and only *then* grab the ends. Now, as you pull your arms through (see fig. 2), the knot will automatically be made for you (see fig. 3). You won't have to do anything else. Except pick out the neon green polka-dot noose your buddy will be sporting tomorrow.

You have to work this through with a tie in your hand. You can't just read the description and think you can make it work on the fly. The effort is worth it as this is one of those things that will become a favorite of yours. —TR

fig. 1

fig. 2

fig. 3

UNDERWATER WAGER

It's a simple bet to make if you're out lunching with coworkers. Wager dessert on whether you can light a match underwater. When your mark takes you up on it, have him hold up a glass of water and then just light a match under the glass. Voilà! It's now "burning underwater." If you do it with a group of coworkers at the table, your mark will feel more foolish debating the technicalities of the cheap scam than just simply springing for the cost of your peanut butter cheesecake.

This is a perfect stunt to pull on a "heat merchant." There's always one person that rubs everyone the wrong way. Sometimes it's the boss, but more often than not, it's a coworker. This is the heat merchant. The emergence of a heat merchant in a work environment is a natural occurrence. Everyone wants this person gone, but if they do go, someone else will emerge as the heat merchant. Just hope that it is not you. The heat merchant (as long as it's not your boss) is the person that should be the target of the pranks and scams presented in this chapter. The bets and cons won't change the fact that the heat merchant gives you grief, but they will allow you to let off some steam and not end up on top of a water tower with a high-powered rifle. —TR

AN IMPORTANT NOTE ABOUT TAKE YOUR GARBAGE TO WORK DAY (PAGE 38)

THE
WALK-AWAY

Be careful with scams like TAKE YOUR GARBAGE TO WORK DAY. Some of your coworkers will start to think that you care. The challenge is to get the right people at your office to think you care. Like if the boss sees you and wants to talk, then talk. If, however, Lonesome Loser Luke (that guy who has lousy social skills and even worse hygiene) wants to be your "bud," use the WALK-AWAY.

The WALK-AWAY gives the impression that you are on your way to an important meeting. When you see Luke coming up to you, and you know he wants to talk (and in doing so suck the life from the marrow of your bones), you walk toward him smiling and then walk past him. If he starts talking to you, turn to face him while slowly walking away backward, as if you want to hear what he has to say but have to get somewhere. Luke will appreciate the attention from someone in such demand and will quickly get to the point of what he has to say (if there is a point). At any moment, you can shoot a quick glance at your watch, grimace, and then give Luke a sheepish smile as you point in the direction you are walking. This is the international sign for "I gotta go!" Smile and make a clean getaway. Repeat as needed.

EMPLOYMENT TIPS
FOR THE
MODERN CON MAN

Most modern con men, yourself included, are not likely to crisscross the country, surviving on wit, instinct, and a newfound knowledge of scamming free drinks. Chances are, you're going to have to go to work. Here are not only some real-world employment tips from actual workers, but also ways that the modern con man lifestyle can come in handy after you've punched out.

ELECTRONICS STORE CLERK

I love working the television department because those things got so many controls. It's not like a video game or some CD, which is either good or just sucks, and either way completely out of my control. TVs come with settings! I make the cheaper ones look like crap—too dark, too contrasty, too washed-out, whatev—then set the more expensive ones to ideal settings. I can talk up the cheap sets all I want, play the customer a little by saying they're really not *that* bad, but in the end the picture quality moves the buyer to where I want them.

Tip for the Modern Con Man: Hey, when you go out to meet girls with a friend, do you bring the best-looking guy you know? Or do you want to be the one getting the attention? Well, that's my attitude when I work the floor . . . and when I walk out the door.

GRAPHIC DESIGNER

When I design catalogs or brochures for events, the most important thing is whether or not there's a section of paid advertising in the back. If so, I tell the client I'll do their job for free as long as I get a full page for myself in the back section. They say fine, as they were expecting to have to go out of pocket for getting the thing designed. Then all I do is break the page into eight sections and sell off the space myself at a higher rate to other businesses. Usually it ends up double what I would've made.

Tip for the Modern Con Man: Life's a flea market. No one knows for sure what the value is of anything. Same goes for you. Walk into a bar and it's up to you to let people know how valuable you are, otherwise they'll set your worth themselves. And since no one knows, by all means exaggerate.

DOOR-TO-DOOR SALESMAN

I sell meat door-to-door and I have this move called the "Turn-and-Talk." See, I keep my meat in the truck, and I figure if I can get the customer to the truck, I can make the sale. It's getting them out of the doorway that's the biggest hurdle. So what I do is, while I'm talking, I turn and begin walking to the truck . . . and I don't stop what I'm saying when I go. Often the customer will step out to listen and follow to hear what I'm saying. Next thing they know, they're looking at my meat.

Tip for the Modern Con Man: How's that apply to life outside the profession? If you wait for someone's approval, it might not come. Assume someone's interested in you and you'd be surprised how often that'll make it come true.

TELEMARKETER

Encyclopedias on CD-ROM are my beat. More often than not, the wife answers the phone. I find the easiest way for a woman to get off the phone is to say she'd have to consult with her husband since it is a rather hefty cost. My go-to response is "I understand. But does your husband consult with you whenever he has to have the car looked at? As the man of the house, I'm sure he has financial things he takes responsibility for. *This* is about your kids and their educations. As the woman of the house, do you really need his approval for that?"

Tip for the Modern Con Man: If you want someone to say yes, make them feel like no is just a reflection of their own weakness, insecurity, or fear. It applies to almost anything, anywhere.

CAR SALESMAN

Everyone knows we've marked up the prices, but no one knows how much. So I can keep repeating "the absolute lowest I can go" as much as I want. I'll even go lower than "my absolute lowest" *just for you.* I make you feel like you're getting a deal—an *insane* deal, a deal in which I'm barely making *anything* anymore—when in fact I'm totally not sweating it. I do this sort of thing all the time.

Tip for the Modern Con Man: You gotta say you don't want to do something even if you do. You pretend you can't do something even when you're planning on doing it . . . like, "You're only free on Thursday? Shoot, I already have plans for Thursday . . . but you know what, I don't want to miss the chance. So let me see if I can reschedule my other thing . . ." Do it with a smile, of course. You're happy to please. If you're happy to please others, they'll be happy to please you. People feel indebted when you seem to bend for them. So loosen up. My tip to you, whenever you can, pretend to bend.

INJURY ATTORNEY

If you're in the hospital with your spine being held together by duct tape and a brace, and I show up, you know it's not just to hand you a get-well-soon card. I like that there's an immediate understanding. I'm looking for gain from your pain. This won't cost you a cent, but if we win, I'm taking a big piece. Nice to meetcha.

Tip for the Modern Con Man: If you get caught doing what you're doing, be up front. If you're hitting on a girl and she calls you on it, say, "Yep, you got me. I wanted to talk to you from the moment you walked in." The weirdest thing is, when you play things like you got nothing to hide, it actually makes you *more* mysterious. People, and I mean women, really dig that.

HOLLYWOOD AGENT

I have five lunch appointments every day, made a month ahead of time. The tide turns fast in this town, and I know that one of the five I'm set to meet with is going to have more mojo than the others. I want the hot person for lunch, and sometimes you don't know who's got the heat til breakfast. My assistant has a lot of last-second apologies to make, but I don't just pay her to get my car cleaned, you know.

Tip for the Modern Con Man: There's no such thing as a sure thing. Even once you find your target—a girl who looks game, a sucker to challenge to pool, it doesn't matter—check out the rest of the room and find alternatives in case something goes wrong. Be nice to everyone you encounter, because not only are you looking for another chump at all times, you might need someone to have your back when the chips start flying.

HOUSE PAINTER

No matter how much I might be asking around for work, if I'm ever asked how I land clients, I always lie and claim it's from referrals and word of mouth: "I honestly don't know how to get new clients. The work's been coming to me for the past few years. I'm kinda embarrassed to say it, but I hardly have to work to get work." It gets them every time.

Tip for the Modern Con Man: The cliché is true, even socially. If you act like you don't need or want it, people are quicker to give it to you.

True friends stab you in the front.
—OSCAR WILDE

CHAPTER 3

"FRIENDLY" WAGERS

Bets with Buddies and Fooling Your Friends

Friends. Where would you be without them? They stick with you through thick and thin. Your job sucks, and your girlfriend hates you. But at least you can always count on your friends, right? No one has more faith in you. Hence, there is no one easier to dupe, flimflam, and take to the cleaners.

MIRROR ME

A fun game you can't lose. And it involves drinking. Drinking and winning.

WHAT IT'S GOOD FOR:
Mocking that pal who always thinks he can top you.

WHAT YOU NEED:
- 2 drinks
- Any random stuff that is lying around

WHAT YOU DO:

1 Challenge your friend to do everything you do. Simple as that. If he can, he wins. If he can't, you win.

2 Proceed to do . . . anything. Pick up a magazine and put it down. Your friend will do the same. Eat a french fry. Your friend will do the same.

3 Take a sip of a drink. Your friend will do the same.

4 Do a few more random things, which he'll repeat.

5 Take a second sip of your drink—a relatively small sip. He'll do the same. **HERE'S THE KEY:** Keep that sip in your mouth.

6 Do a couple more random moves and then spit that last sip back into the glass. He'll have swallowed, of course, and will not be able to do the same last thing you did.

7 Make fun of him by saying you heard he likes to swallow.

CONFIDENTIAL FRIENDSHIPS

If a man wearing a pinkie ring offers to make a bet with you, walk away. You may have already known this: Human beings have a strong sense of instinct. What you may not have known is what exactly the pinkie ring means in the world of the grifter. Con men have been wearing expensive pinkie rings for a long time, originally to help their friends out of a specific and unfortunate financial quandary should a dark day arrive. See, if the swindler in question were to meet a sudden end, he wouldn't want to saddle his pals with the burden of paying for a burial. Hence, the pinkie ring, which was to be pawned to cover the cost.

These days, you can still see a bunch of old-timers with pinkie rings hanging out in the afternoons at the Farmers Market in Los Angeles, corner of Fairfax and Third. You might see them, but steer clear, especially if one of them tells you he can bite his eye. —TR

A LATE-NIGHT SWINDLE

If it's late, here's a way you might be able to make ten bucks off your tired friend. Offer up twenty bucks and have your pal do the same. Place both bills inside a matchbox and offer to sell him the forty dollars for just thirty. If you do it quick—added, hopefully, to his fatigue and, if you're lucky, drunkenness—he might think he's getting a bargain. In fact, you'll be the only one profiting.

THE HOT HAND

Another fun challenge. The loser might feel some pain, so it's best to do this with friends. Because if you can't burn your friends, who can you burn?

WHAT IT'S GOOD FOR:
Winner picks what you'll watch on TV.

WHAT YOU NEED:
• Matches

WHAT YOU DO:

1 Challenge a friend to hold a lit match upside down for twenty seconds. Or you can say, "Whoever holds it upside down the longest wins." Because either way, you're going to win.

2 Let your friend go first. He'll feel his fingertips burning after four or five seconds tops and drop the match.

3 Okay, your turn, and here's the trick: While keeping the match upside down, slowly move your hand from left to right, continually moving it back and forth. The movement will make the flame smaller, and it won't burn your fingers unless you stop. The bet was simply to keep the match upside down. You did that. You also won.

When the mark loses, he has no one to blame but himself. After all, his mother told him, "Never play with matches." She wasn't talking about fire safety. This is what she meant.

These bits of deception are good because anyone can do them. Like so much of this material, the mark knows he's getting an education and will probably do it to someone else. Deceit: It's the gift that keeps on giving. —TR

HOW TO START A CULT

Friends are nice, but followers are better. An easy way to build a flock is with demonstrations of psychic ability. It's not hard, but you will need an oracle. An oracle is anything that will supposedly put you in touch with the wonders of the universe. You have to "read" something, like palms or cards or crystals or tea leaves or anything. It doesn't matter. We know one guy that does, believe it or not, vagina readings. Man, we wish we had thought of that. It's pure genius.

So you have whatever you have to look at, you stare at it intently, mutter a few things like "Hmm, that's interesting," and then launch into the reading. As to what you say, this should give you some ideas:

- I get a sense about you that you are someone with a strong personality and a generally positive outlook. You deal with others openly, but this has resulted in your being hurt and disappointed in the past. You are more cautious now in revealing yourself to others, but you still could be called a giving person. As a matter of fact, I feel you find it easier to give than to take from others.

- Because of your generosity of spirit, you have made acquaintances and yet few close friends. I get a sense that when you do become fond of someone, you go all out for them. As I concentrate on this area, I keep flashing on the word *loyalty*. I believe this is what you offer to others and what you value when it is returned.

- On the other side of this is the fact that solitude is important to you. I feel this comes from earlier in life. As a child, you often felt you were misunderstood and on your own, and by the time you were fifteen or sixteen, you were your own person. The word *independent* keeps coming to me.

- The inner strength you have surprises some people, and some don't notice, for they don't see the real you. Your flexibility is useful in dealing with situations. You also have a tendency to be self-critical. Sometimes you get angry with yourself when you put off doing tasks that are unpleasant. Sometimes you get frustrated when you realize that you have a great deal of unused potential that you have yet to turn to your advantage.

- You have made a number of trips in the past. Short trips involving other people. There is more travel in the future. Your presence and attention will be needed in a distant location in the future, not too long from now. The number six comes to me, but I can't clearly say what this means.

- You pride yourself in being an independent thinker, and you are often sought out by others for your advice. I feel that has happened twice just recently. On the other hand, you sometimes don't value your judgment enough and go along with other people just to avoid confrontation. You did this a while back, and it resulted in you not reaching for the brass ring.

- Currently you're at a crossroads. The way is not clear. What is required now is patience and clear thinking. Like a good poker player, you must make the most of the cards you have been dealt.

- I feel that you have trouble saying no at times when you should. Still, I see some improvement in this area. Also, in the future, you will receive some unexpected news, and money will be coming your way.

- Romantically, things have not always been the easiest. Your sexual adjustment has presented some problems for you. I sense a number of people in your past but only one really special relationship. In the future is an extended period of contentment and happiness involving a close, rewarding relationship that grows and builds all the way through. It might not be exactly what you expect, so keep yourself open emotionally.

- Your greatest asset is a positive mind-set. You are a creative person with a strong imagination. You need a certain amount of change and variety in your life and become dissatisfied when hemmed in by restrictions and limitations. Especially when others impose them needlessly on you. Your creative mind allows you to look at things as they should be, and this will be a powerful motivating factor as you progress through life.

- I get a feeling that as the years go by, you will continue to grow as a person, and because of this, you will grow older but never grow old.

- There have been ups and downs in your life, but I feel the major challenges and difficulties are behind you. Take a lesson from the artist who steps back from his canvas to get a broad perspective of the entire picture. If you can do this with your life, you will see what needs to be done to pursue the positive, avoid the negative, and live a productive and fulfilling life. Your future is bright, and happiness will be yours.

After hitting them with all of the above, the mark will bow down and kiss the hem of your garment. You'll have a worshipper. And that can be so much better (and more profitable) than having a friend.

MENTAL PREPAREDNESS

You can work long and hard on cardsharping or pickpocketing or any of a thousand other skills that can be used to fleece others, but there is one skill that is the most important of them all. To scam people you have to be able to lie. And do it well. Very well. The good news is that it's not hard, and like so many things in life, the more you do it, the easier it becomes.

The key is convincing yourself that what you are saying is true. This shouldn't seem too challenging once you realize you've been telling yourself lies for years. Not only that—you've been falling for them! (See, you're pretty good at this already.) You tell yourself that everything will work out when you probably suspect it won't. You've convinced yourself that she probably would've gone home with you if only you'd made a move, that your clothes don't smell, and that the other guys weren't mocking you last night—they actually did think you were funny. Odds are you aren't even as good looking as you think (although if your self-esteem sucks, you may actually be better looking, but you clearly have other issues to deal with). In other words, you've had a lifetime of practicing the most important skill you need. This is good news.

So I'm not asking you to stop all this self-deception. No, I'm just saying that what you have to do now is take this skill of lying to yourself that you've unknowingly perfected and share it with your fellow man.

It's all about giving.

TWICE-BURNT
WITH THE "THRICE-BURNT" REHASH

Here's a nasty way to follow up the HOT HAND—if you're really feeling risky. Take the match that's already been lit and blown out, and bet that you can make that very match burn again. If your friend takes you up on it, just hold a lighter to the end of the match and relight it. And now the match is *burning again*.

There's a way to do a quick rehash on this, *to make it burn a third time*.

While the match is still burning, claim that you can blow it out and make it burn a third time without the help of a lighter or another match or any sort of flame. If your pal takes you up on it, just blow out the match and immediately touch it to his arm. He'll flinch and say you burned him. And yep, that's the match "burning" a third time.

As they say: Burn me once, shame on you. Burn me twice, shame on me. Burn me three times, I'm a freaking moron.

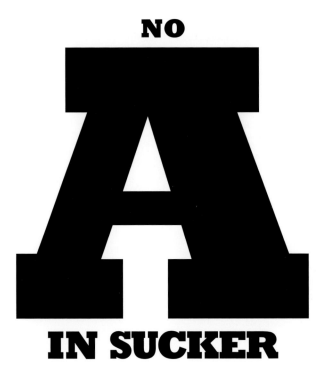

NO **A** IN SUCKER

Here's an easy way to make someone else beat your friend in a simple wager.

WHAT IT'S GOOD FOR:
The double bonus of impressing a girl and making your friend seem like a dope.

WHAT YOU NEED:
- 2 people

WHAT YOU DO:
1 Bet your buddy that the girl will be able to say fifty words that don't include the letter *a*—in under twenty seconds and without any planning. Even the girl, when you finally explain the bet to her, will be doubtful of her ability to pull that off. Which will make her appreciate you more when she does.

2 So that your buddy doesn't hear, whisper these three little words to her: "Count to fifty."

3 Okay, you might want to add a fourth word: "Quickly!"

WHAT'S THE SECRET:
No spelled-out number between one and nine hundred ninety-nine has an *a* in it. (And don't be one of those dopes who incorrectly puts an "and" in numbers, like "one hundred and twelve.") If you want to eliminate the twenty-second limit, you can even say you can rattle off a thousand words without the letter *a*. Just go ahead and count to a thousand—making sure that after nine hundred ninety-nine, you finish with the thousandth word: "Done."

WHO'S YOUR BUDDY?

When old-school grifters attempted to pull off long, elaborate cons, the trick was to first become friends with the mark. Well, not a real friend, but the kind of friend who has no problem taking the other guy for all he's worth and sending him down the river barefoot and broke.*

While there are no such "long cons" taught in this book (and we're not advocating any—although if you play it right, CEO SLAVE can last for a while), it's worth noting that the process of turning an acquaintance into a friend is the important first step before turning him into a sucker. So here are some easy pointers to get the buddy ball rolling and the friendship flag flying:

1   Confide in him with some secret. "I've never told anyone this before . . ."

2   If he's short some money, help him out. (A small amount. I mean, who's the sucker here?) When he tries to repay, tell him to forget it.

3   Find out his nickname and use it often. If he doesn't have one, create a harmless one. "Ace" always works.

4   Set him up with a girl.

5   Call him, depressed. "Got a minute? I just need to talk to someone."

6   When introducing him, begin with "My good buddy . . ."

7   Subtly mention different local teams until he takes the bait— most guys love to talk at least one sport.

8   "Hey, I've had enough. You want this donut/cookie/slice of pizza/bong hit?"

9   Enlist him to help with one of those minor bets we've given you.

10   "Nice shirt!"

But the inexperienced con man always runs a risk with this method. What happens if he and the mark actually start *being* friends? What happens if he really starts to care? Going on fishing trips . . . *for fun*? He knows the sucker is good for $100K, but then the guy lets slip that the wife's about to leave him and how he's still paying the hospital for his old motorcycle injury . . . The grifter knows he needs to learn as much about the mark as possible—but suddenly he starts getting the whole sob story and has a hard time pulling the proverbial trigger on the operation. Another perfectly good sting slips away.

Just to be safe, here are a few warning signs to watch out for—to let you know if you're getting too close:

1   The mark knows where you live.

2   The mark knows your real name.

3   The mark knows how you like your eggs in the morning and how much starch you want in your collar.

4   He's on your Christmas card list.

5   You've swapped recipes.

6   You've swapped spit.

7   Cat sitting.

---

* This notion might be confusing to you if you're the kind of person who thinks you have 3,643 friends because you've "poked" 3,641 people you've never met on Facebook.

FACE DOWN

With FACE DOWN, your friend will have to "face up" to a simple fact: He's a loser. You'll also drive him crazy as you continue to do something seemingly easy that he just can't figure out.

WHAT IT'S GOOD FOR:
Choosing who makes the next beer run at your pal's house party.

WHAT YOU NEED:
• 3 empty shot glasses

WHAT YOU DO:
1   Arrange the three glasses in a row—the first one face up, the second one face down, and the third one face up.

2   In three moves (no more and no fewer) your mark has to get all three glasses in the face-down position. On each move, the player has to flip two of the glasses—from down to up or up to down. When your mark fails miserably, you're up to bat.

3   Here are your three turns (a, b, and c):

a) Turn over the second and third glasses.
Now the first is face up, the second is face up, and the third is face down.

b) Turn over the first and third.
Now the first is face down, the second is face up, and the third is face up.

c) Turn over the second and third again.
Now the first is face down, the second is face down, and the third is face down.

(continued)

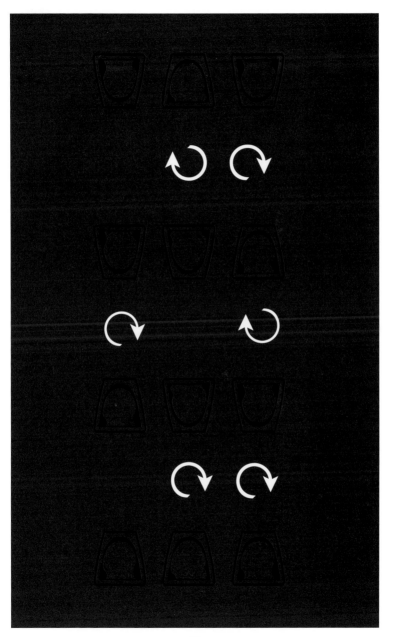

WHAT ELSE YOU SHOULD KNOW:

There's a more evil way to play this game, which just so happens to be our preferred method. It's also the only reason we're including it here at all.

1 Do the exact setup as before. (Don't call too much attention to the way the glasses are set up; just say, "We position them like so," and move on to the instructions.)

2 Demonstrate how it's done—quickly—so your mark can see it *can* actually be done.

3 Then, with all the cups in the face-down position (you just showed how it's done), "reset" the cups . . . but this time, do so by just turning the middle one face up (see fig. 1). If you notice, this is the exact *opposite* of how you set it up originally. Say, "Now you do it."

4 He won't be able to from this setup. And when he gives up, reset the cups, but this time the right way, and do it for him again.

fig. 1

When the mark is taking his turn, I like to utter little bits of encouragement like "Good. There you go. Okay. That's it." I do this in a half voice and don't make a big deal about it. When he fails, I hide my joy and spill out a slightly perplexed "Huh? Let's try that again." This keeps the momentum going and continues the mark on his path of losing. I picked up this subtlety from a jointee called Savannah Mike at the old Nu-Pike amusement park in Long Beach, California. —TR

WHO SAYS THERE'S NO SUCH THING AS A FREE LUNCH?

Here's one way of getting a free meal (or even making a few bucks) when a bunch of friends go out to eat. When the check comes, just wait until a number of people have put in their money. Then look at the bill, pretend to add up your portion, and just put in a single dollar. Move the check along. If you get away with this, great. If someone sees you do it, though, claim you were just joking. Take the dollar back, put a ten-dollar bill into the pot, and remove a twenty. If you get away with this, then you not only got a free meal, you made ten bucks. If someone calls you on this, again claim you were joking, put the twenty back in, and remove a ten-dollar bill—which should appear as though you're adding the difference (ten bucks) to the total. Then ask the mark if he's happy now. He says yes and you have just gotten a free meal.

OL'
DOC SHANNON

This chapter seems like the right place to talk about a man who was a dear friend to many young grifters: Ol' Doc Shannon. He got his start back in the 1930s working the tail end of the medicine show business. He worked with Doc Bartok and had a hand in a number of Hadacol promotions. When he started, he was known as Young Doc Shannon, and came into his later moniker as the years wore on.

When the med show industry dried up, which had something to do with the government not being pleased with the fact that the patent medicine did nothing, he switched over to doing jam auctions. He was well versed in all manner of grift, but the jam auction was the thing that kept him from ever missing a meal.

One time back in the 1970s, Shannon was driving north through the great state of North Carolina on his way to playing a spot in Virginia. He was driving his lovely old 1959 cream-colored Cadillac sedan. It was about ten o'clock at night.

He was about five miles from the border when he noticed the dreaded cherry lights in his rearview mirror. He wasn't speeding ("Only rush if there is a reason," he used to say), so he wasn't sure why he was being pulled over. Doc took a quick mental inventory to see if there was a possible warrant that he had forgotten to square. Nothing came to mind, except for a minor indiscretion a few years past involving an overly amorous bearded lady while he was working as the outside talker of the Kelly-Miller sideshow. He doubted that she would call in the local constabulary, so he truly didn't know why he was being stopped.

The highway patrolman approached the car, and as Doc rolled down the window, he gave the cop a gentle smile and said, "Good evening, Officer. How can I be of service to you?"

The stone-faced lawman said, "You have a taillight out."

"Yes, I know. I am on my way to get it fixed" was Doc's reply.

"That shit don't fly with me. You're getting a ticket," said the trooper, with noticeable tension in his jaw.

"Is it possible to just get a warning?"

"Nope." The cop took out his ticket book.

Doc, realizing that it was the end of the month and this incident had more to do with meeting a ticket quota than public safety, began to seethe. After a moment of silence, Doc spoke.

"Officer, may I ask you a question?"

The trooper didn't look up from his writing, but he nodded.

"Thank you. If I were to call you an asshole, what would you do?"

This got the cop's attention. He stopped writing, looked at Doc with animosity in his eyes, and answered with more than a bit of edge in his voice, "I'd bounce you into jail."

Doc, the epitome of politeness continued, "But if I just *think* you are an asshole, what can you do?"

"Nothing" was the answer from the man in blue.

"I see. Then I *think* you are an asshole."

The highway man stood there for a long spell and just glared at Doc. He then closed his ticket book and with quiet venom said, "Get the hell out of my state."

"With pleasure, Officer, with pleasure" was Doc's final comment to the policeman.

Ol' Doc Shannon then rolled up his window and made haste northward on Highway 95.

ASHLESS WONDER

Bet your pal a buck you can light a cigarette and smoke it, but that there'll be no ash and it won't get any shorter. The solution is simple: Don't light the end of the cigarette—light the middle. Then take a drag and exhale in his face, punctuating the point that you won and he lost. Take another drag and blow a smoke ring for flair. But don't bother with a third puff. It's time to collect your money.

GRIFTER HISTORY

PART 1

The Dawn of Man to the Nineteenth Century

Deception got an early start, when the serpent conned Eve into eating the apple in the Garden of Eden. It was an effective con, as it left the victims naked and homeless. Roughly one testament after this herpetological bunco, Christ himself warned of biblical bar bettors: "By smooth talk and flattery they deceive the minds of naive people" (Romans 16:17–18). The advice apparently did not reach the Trojans, who a few years later fell for the mother of all bait-and-switch tactics, the gift horse. And in the first century AD, a temple designed by the Greek inventor Heron featured a primitive hydraulic system to magically open the temple doors. This impressed and scared the daylights out of followers and kept the shekels from the congregation flowing into the coffers of the temple priests. And you thought TV evangelists fleecing their flocks was something new?

But the con became an art form with the birth of these United States. H. L. Mencken put it best when he wrote, "The men the American people admire most extravagantly are the most daring liars; the men they detest most violently are those who try to tell them the truth." Starry-eyed dreamers set loose in a land of potential riches were ideal marks. Suddenly it seemed that there really was a sucker born every minute, and a new breed of grifter cropped up to take advantage of this wondrous land of infinite possibilities. Following are a few notable examples.

WILLIAM THOMPSON (?–1849)

Thompson was a New York criminal whose exploits caused the coining of the term "confidence man." He simply asked an upper-class mark, "Have you confidence in me to trust me with your watch until tomorrow?" If the answer was yes, Thompson disappeared with the watch and would not be seen again. His ploy was weak by today's standards, but hey, you have to start somewhere. By the 1860s, police estimated that one out of ten criminals in New York was a confidence man. Of course, this estimate did not include the police themselves, even though every cop in New York at that time was on the take.

GEORGE DEVOL (1826–1903)

With his partner, Canada Bill, DeVol spent decades and made a fortune fleecing suckers on riverboats and trains with three-card monte. He and Bill both died penniless because as fast as they would make their money, they would lose it again playing the game faro (see page 102). There's a famous story about their obsession: One night in Baton Rouge, DeVol found Bill being taken at a rigged game of faro. DeVol took Bill aside and said, "Can't you see this game is crooked?" "Sure I know it, George," sighed Bill with resignation, "but it's the only game in town."

JEFFERSON "SOAPY" SMITH (1860–1898)

Smith crossed west through our still-innocent country with a gang, performing three-card monte, the shell game, and other short cons. He briefly exhibited a petrified man nicknamed McGinty for the price of ten cents per peek. He used the gimmick to bring victims to him, instead of having to find them himself. While customers waited in line with dimes in their hands, Soapy's short cons were winning the dollars out of their pockets. For over twenty years he led the most infamous crew of swindlers ever assembled, the Soap Gang. The memory of Soapy is honored every year with a birthday party hosted by his great-grandson at the famous Magic Castle club in Hollywood.

CASSIE CHADWICK (1859–1907)

Chadwick passed herself off as the illegitimate daughter of the richest bachelor in the world, Andrew Carnegie. Believing her, banks and other millionaires lent her obscene amounts of money—somewhere between two and twenty million dollars. She was the ruin of several financial institutions and the downfall of prominent leaders of industry. When she was finally arrested, the cops found her lounging in bed wearing a money belt containing one hundred thousand dollars. She died in jail two years later at the age of forty-eight.

JOSEPH "YELLOW KID" WEIL (1875–1976)

Weil began grifting when he was seventeen, when he noticed that his coworkers at a collection agency were keeping small sums for themselves. He promised them he wouldn't snitch for a share of the loot. Then, under the tutelage of Chicago con man Doc Meriwether, Weil started performing short cons in the 1890s at public sales of Meriwether's Elixir, the chief ingredient of which was rainwater. Over the course of his career, Weil became one of the most famous American confidence men of his era and is said to have taken more than eight million dollars. He lived to 100 and was still scamming to the end.

HOW "SOAPY" SMITH GOT HIS NAME

"How are you fixed for soap?" was the line that Jefferson Smith used to rope in suckers for his pitch as he sold soap on a busy corner. In the late 1870s, Smith conned large crowds with a trick later known as the Prize Package Soap Sell Swindle. First, he publicly wrapped currency, from one dollar to one hundred dollars, around a few of the soap bars, and then wrapped them all in plain paper. After mixing up all the packages (those with money inside and those without), Smith would tell the crowd that he was selling the bars for a dollar each. A shill would buy the first bar, tear it open, and excitedly announce that he had won a dollar, showing his winnings to all. The soap would sell fast, each buyer hoping to get the still-unclaimed hundred-dollar bill. Many victims would buy several bars. Through sleight of hand, of course, the money-wrapped soap was removed before the selling even began. Soapy Smith "cleaned up" with this bit for over two decades.

Look around the table. If you don't see a sucker, get up, because you are the sucker.
—AMARILLO SLIM

CHAPTER 4

Poker Night Games and Other Ways to Con a Card Player

Conning while card playing can be the move of a dumbass. You're already looking at an evening of bluffing, suspicion, and blank, ungiving faces staring you back. It might even seem that there's no worse time for a con than when the cards have been dealt, the chips tossed in, and everyone's wearing their best poker face. Well, guess again. A little creativity and well-placed maliciousness can tip the balance of the night in your favor, and maybe, just maybe, there's no *better* setup for a con artist with a catalog of tricks. Forget about poker and trying to master the technique for bottom-dealing. Because when the other chumps around the table are playing poker, you just play them. Trust us, there are many more ways to win at cards than just with the hand you've been dealt.

AUSTRALIAN BLACKJACK

As blackjack is also known as twenty-one, this version might be called thirty-one. This dirty little no-lose game from Down Under is a card-playing variation on NIM that guarantees the same wonderful result.

WHAT IT'S GOOD FOR:
When you want to take a break from poker but not take a break from winning.

WHAT YOU NEED:
• 6 playing cards—ace through six (suits don't matter)

WHAT YOU DO:
1   Line up the ace through six in a row, faceup.

2   Make sure you wager a few valuable chips.

3   Now you and your mark take turns pointing to a card and adding it to the total value.

4   The only rule: You can't pick the same card that the other person just pointed to.

5   Continue adding until someone's pick takes the total value to thirty-one. Whoever does, wins. Whoever doesn't, or goes over, loses.

WHAT'S THE SECRET:

1   There are key numbers you're aiming to hit on your turn. If you miss the first, you can go for the second or third one. The numbers are three, ten, seventeen, and twenty-four (if you go first, point to the three and the rest is in the bag).

2   Once you hit one of the magic numbers, just make sure your mark's choice plus your choice equals seven. So if you start with three and he picks two, you go with five. Then you're at ten. If he then picks the three, you point to the four. You're at seventeen. And so on. Soon you'll be able to hit thirty-one.

GET EVEN
WITH ODDS

The odds are 1 in 147,717 that your cause of death will be dog attack. The odds of that hot girl at the end of the bar giving you her phone number? Significantly better. The point here is that we're playing the percentages every day of our lives in one way or another. Here are a few quick card wagers in which the odds are in your favor, though your mark will assume the opposite. Will you win every time? No. But if you lose, go double or nothing. It's mathematically certain that you'll win *most* of the time. Besides, you can always get back to the game of poker and play the odds there, since you're more likely to get a royal flush in the opening hand (1 in 649,739) than die from flesh-eating bacteria (1 in 1 million).

1

Ask the mark to name two cards. Any two. Suits don't matter. For example, let's say he names a four and a nine. Bet that you'll find those cards right next to each other in a deck. He'll take the bet—so would you. But take a deck and rifle through it. Odds are you'll find those two cards together.

2

Ask your mark to cut the deck into three face-down piles. Bet that if you turn over the top card in each pile, one of them will be a face card. The odds are heavily in your favor.

3

Take three black cards and two red cards. Shuffle them and lay them down in a row, facedown. Challenge your mark to turn over two cards without turning over a red card. He'll take the bet—there are more black cards, right? Seems like he has the safer bet, but he doesn't. The odds are that one will be red.

OUT FROM UNDER

If you have an empty beer bottle on the table and a buck in your pocket, then go ahead and turn over the bottle and balance it on the dollar. The challenge to your mark is to get the dollar out from under it, without touching the bottle and without knocking it over. We suggest doing this when your mark might feel rushed, like if you have a one-minute break while a third player is hitting the head. This will work to your favor since the solution takes patience: rolling up the dollar from one end and slowly continuing even as the roll reaches the bottle. Keep it up—very gently and steadily—and let the roll lightly slide the bottle off the end of the dollar.*

---

* The authors of this book do not explicitly recommend practicing with rolling paper.

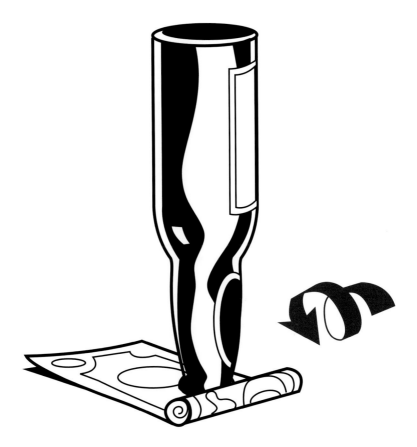

THE BEST HAND

Here's a way to give your draw poker opponent every opportunity to win, which will make his eventual loss that much more embarrassing. It's a bet that seems impossible for your mark to lose. Unfortunately, impossible isn't good enough odds for him.

WHAT IT'S GOOD FOR:

Taking down the guy who's feeling lucky that night and messing with his mojo.

WHAT YOU NEED:
• A deck of cards

WHAT YOU DO:

1 Challenge the mark to a game of draw poker in which each player gets to handpick his cards from a face-up deck. And the mark can go second, therefore seeing your hand and deciding how to beat it before he selects his. Seems too good to be true, right?*

2 Turn a deck over and spread out the cards so everyone can see them.

3 Make your hand: a four of a kind, using the four tens, and a king kicker.

4 Now it's his turn. If he knows what he's doing, he'll probably take the four aces (a superior four of a kind to yours) and then some fifth card.

5 Since it's draw poker, you can now discard. You choose to discard three cards: three of your tens.

6 Now take three new cards needed to build a king-high straight flush with your king and remaining ten—the queen, jack, and nine of the same suit as the king and ten in your hand.

7 He won't be able to do the same, since you've discarded the other tens. Your current hand beats his and anything else he can create. His magic is gone. He is a loser.

---

* It is.

Remember Nick the Greek, the legendary gambler who was reputed to have won two hundred thousand dollars with the game NIM? Well, there was a game that managed to take him for over four million dollars. And the name of that game was poker. —TR

LEAP OF FAITH

People can take cards so seriously. Sometimes too seriously. If you have someone like that at the table, a good way to undermine his focus is with something completely out of left field and silly. Take this bet, for instance: that you'll put a card down somewhere around the table and he won't be able to jump over it. You're not going to touch him, interfere, or place it against the wall or on a high ledge. When he takes you up on it, simply lay the card down on the top of his head.

WHAT ARE YOU ?

It's important to know what you are so when someone calls you a name you know whether or not the accuser is correct (either way, feel free to throw a chair in his direction).

Case in point is the term *card shark*. What is a card shark? Well, think of a pool shark. He's the guy who beats lesser players by seeming to be beneath *them*. He plays fair (that is, by the rules) but manipulates the situation by changing the mark's perception of who he is and what he can do. Technically speaking, you wouldn't call him a cheater (well, maybe you would, in which case we recommend ducking fast). The pool shark still wins on skill. In the end, he simply puts the balls in the pockets, one after the other, before the mark does.*

A card shark is the same thing, but with cards. He doesn't cheat. He doesn't use a marked deck, deal from the bottom, or count cards. He's not shooting signals to his buddy across the way or carrying an extra ace up his sleeve. He's simply controlling the game by manipulating others' perceptions of him. Whether he's playing dumb, inexperienced, distracted, or what have you, he's still playing on the square with the cards he's been given and making the most of them.

Don't confuse a *card shark* with a *card sharp*. The card sharp is a mechanic and uses skill to do all the things listed in the above paragraph (and more) to win. In short, the card sharp is a cheat. It's as simple as that. Not that there's anything wrong with that. We are what we are, and should take pride in what we do, as long as we do it well.

---

* Pool sharks are known to be rather fond of this label, going so far as to refer to marks as "fish."

NO-LOSE
POKER

Here's a stripped-down game of poker that's played with ten cards. "No-Lose" refers to you and your chances. All things considered, from the other guy's perspective, "No-Win" is more like it. And while this might seem really complicated at first, it's not. We're just being overly thorough for the slow ones out there.

WHAT IT'S GOOD FOR:

Taking down the other three players at the table, one at a time. Note: There are three variations on this, so after you beat the first mark, move on to the second. Then get the third. And always make sure you're betting.

WHAT YOU NEED:

• A deck of cards

WHAT YOU MUST DO BEFORE PHASE ONE:

1 Before you propose playing, secretly create a stack of ten cards. First, make three sets of three. Say, three jacks, three fours, and three queens.

2 Add an odd-man-out card, the tenth. We'll use a king. This odd-man-out card is known as the Jonah card. In order to know that this is the Jonah card when it's facedown, make sure it has a slight mark on it. The slightest. Either a tiny dot or fold or smudge. Whatever it is (natural or man-made) should be hardly noticeable—except to you.

3 Take these ten cards, making sure the Jonah card is on the bottom, and put that ten-card slug on the top of the other forty-two cards in the deck. Now you're ready.

PHASE ONE:

1   Suggest a sudden-death one-hand version of poker.

2   Say, "We need ten cards," and quickly deal out the top ten cards onto the table in a new tiny stack. The tenth card should be your previously marked Jonah card.

3   Put the other forty-two cards aside. You won't be playing with those.

4   Have your mark shuffle this pile of ten cards until he is happy.

5   Take the cards back and say, "Just lemme make sure there are ten here." (This is why you should act quick and casual in step two, making it seem later like you may have accidentally taken eleven or only nine.)

6   As you count the cards in the shuffled minideck, what you're actually doing is looking for the mark on the Jonah card. Note its position as you count. When you're done, say, "Yep, ten cards."

7   If the Jonah is in an "odd position"—meaning the first, third, fifth, seventh, or ninth card—then *you* do the dealing. This insures that he will get the Jonah card.

8   If it's in an "even position"—the second, fourth, sixth, eighth, or tenth card—you hand the mark the deck and say, "Now deal us each a hand." *He* deals. This again insures that *he* will get the Jonah card.

9   Whoever has the Jonah card (the mark) will end up with the inferior hand.

10 Whoever doesn't (you) will have the winning hand. It just works out that way.*

(continued)

---

* If he has a pair, you'll have a three of a kind. If he has a three of a kind, you will have a full house.

PHASE TWO:

Having just won, turn to mark number two and say, "Let's play again, but we'll do it a little differently this time."

1   Hand him the ten cards so he can shuffle them first. But this time have him shuffle them by moving them around on the table, facedown. Make sure he spreads them around, mixing them up and sliding them all over the table.

2   Now, without dealing, the players just alternate taking cards, until each holds a hand of five. No one gets dealt cards in this phase.

3   Go first by taking a card as you explain what's happening, and make sure you don't take the Jonah card. By avoiding it on your first move, you guarantee he'll get stuck with the Jonah in the end.

4   As you know, whoever holds the Jonah loses. So you win phase two.**

PHASE THREE:

1   This is a lot like phase two, but this time you put the cards *face up* on the table.

2   Again, just take the first card as you explain, making sure you don't take the Jonah (the king).

3   Your hand will beat his.

** In phase two, if you see the mark take the Jonah card on his first move, you can act really crazy, lean back, and say, "To make things even *more* interesting, why don't you pick my cards for me." No matter what he gives you, he'll *still* lose.

THE CON ARTIST'S ARTIST

This might seem like a strange chapter in which to talk about fine art, but since a grifter can only benefit from knowing a little about everything, it certainly can't hurt. Besides, you'll see that card playing is the perfect segue into the visual arts, a world that— certainly in regard to the contemporary art market—seems like the biggest scam going.

Of course, when you hear someone described as the "con artist's artist," you might think of Pablo Picasso, who told us that "bad artists copy, great artists steal," or Marcel Duchamp, who decided that a discarded urinal was art in 1917 and changed what the word has meant ever since.

But you'd be wrong. Because who we're really talking about is, of course, Cassius Marcellus Coolidge (1844–1934), the man known as Cash to friends and family. Untrained as a painter, he was the genius who gave us a series of oil paintings called Dogs Playing Poker, which depict—you guessed it—dogs playing poker. And no proper poker room today is complete without a framed reproduction.

While these paintings have been imitated time and time again, don't be fooled. The one you're considering with the dogs playing pool? Not a Coolidge! And if you discover you have lucked upon or inherited one of the originals (say, *A Bold Bluff* or *Looks Like Four of a Kind*), we strongly discourage a casual discard. After all, in 2005, two paintings from the series sold for a surprising $590,400.

Reminds me of a story this friend of mine told me. He was walking by a lobby table in the Grand Goose Hotel in Ruffled Muff, Texas, and noticed three men and a dog playing cards. Remarkably, the dog was running the show. He shuffled, dealt, and played well enough to stay in the game. "That's a pretty smart dog," my friend remarked. "Nah, he's not that smart," one of the other players whispered back. "Every time he gets a good hand he wags his tail." —TR

THE FARO PHENOMENON

If ESPN had existed in the eighteenth and nineteenth centuries, there would have been nonstop airings of *The World Series of Faro*, no doubt featuring celebrity drop-ins by the likes of composer/heartthrob Franz Liszt and French author Alexandre Dumas (who'd be using the opportunity to plug his new book, *The Count of Monte Cristo*). The wildly popular card game probably got its name from *pharaoh*, as French playing cards of that era were decorated with Egyptian symbols.

A game of faro could involve any number of players. The thirteen cards of one suit, from ace to king, were laid in a row, faceup on a table. Each player placed money on one of the cards. Think of it as a card-playing variation on roulette, but instead of spinning a wheel, the banker drew two cards from the rest of the deck—a banker card and a player card.

If the banker card was, say, a six and a player had put down money on the six, then the banker collected the money. But if a player had put down money on the six and the player card turned out to be a six, the banker paid out *double* the bet. Odds for the players were quite good, and only a couple of rules benefited the banker (such as in cases when both the banker and player cards turned out to be the same). In other words, it was not unheard of for bankers to cheat.

But the game was eventually outlawed in France, as critics found it addictive, shady, and harmful to families and finances. It continued to thrive, however, in England and especially the United States, where "addictive, shady, and harmful to families and finances" describes so much of our wonderful lifestyle. In the Old West, a saloon without a faro game was like a saloon without bottles smashing and toothless whores. In the end, though—while simple, fast paced, and easy to win—faro eventually faded away as poker grew more and more popular. By the 1940s, the game had virtually disappeared.

FOUR LESSONS ON . . .

WHEN GOOD CONS GO BAD

If you follow the instructions you find on these pages, these scams and cons will *never* fail. Yeah, I know, that's a lie. Hey, this book is full of lies. So what's one more?

Okay, what do you do if it all falls apart? Well, that depends on how bad the situation is. If you lose a bet, laugh and pay up. This is not such a bad thing as it makes the mark feel like he is immortal, and pride comes before the fall. Move on to another scam and make back what you lost the first time.

Sometimes losing is not the problem. You win but the mark is a sore loser and beefs about what has happened. You can try chilling him out by buying him a drink and explaining that now he can do the same scam on someone else. The odds are that this whiner will be enough of a weasel to see the benefit and shut the hell up.

Rarely does a scene turn really ugly, but you never can know for sure how something will turn out. Be prepared. Always examine the exit and find out if there are bars on the windows of the bathrooms and, if not, whether you would be able to haul your ass through that portal if need be.

If the worst-case scenario should arise, there are a number of things to do. If a loser should come toward you with harmful intent, scream as loud and long as you can. This can be very disconcerting for an assailant, will get the attention of everyone in the room, and may give you the opportunity to run like the wind to the exit or bathroom while the loser is trying to figure out what the hell is going on.

If escape is not an option, feign fear and hold your hands up like you don't want to fight. Then kick him in the groin as hard as you can. We fight fast and we fight dirty. Once out, I would recommend that you not only leave the immediate vicinity, but also that city, perhaps even that state, and maybe even that country. It's not that hard to change one's name and get a new social security number. You don't think I have always been (or always will be) Todd Robbins, do you?

THE
POSEIDON

You already have a deck of cards. Would it kill you to know one damn trick that doesn't totally suck?

WHAT IT'S GOOD FOR:
Breaking the tension and looking amazing in the process.

WHAT YOU NEED:
• A deck of cards

WHAT YOU DO:

1   Fan the cards and have the mark select one.

2   Turn your back so he can show the card around.

3   Turn to face him again and have him slide the card, facedown, back into the deck, somewhere in the middle.

4   Ask the mark to look you in the eye and say some magic word, like "orgasm."

5   Once your mark says it, spread the deck out, and your mark's card will be the only face-up one in the deck.

6   Remove the card and start a religion.

WHAT'S THE SECRET:

1   When you turn your back to the group and they're looking at his card, you square up the deck, turn the deck upside down, and turn the top card facedown.

2   You then turn around and face your public. The deck will look like all the cards are face-down, but that ain't the case. Only the top card is. All the cards under it are face-up.

3   Now we're at the point where the mark slides the chosen card facedown into the deck, looks you dead in the eye, and utters the magic word. While the mark is in a stare-down with you, he is *not looking at the deck*. That's when you casually flip the deck over so the top is now the bottom. (Hence the name Poseidon—the deck is upside down.) It helps to dip the deck down as you ask him for that magic word. This takes the heat off the deck.

4   All that's left to do: Don't let the bottom card show as you're spreading out the deck to reveal that face-up card.

You want to avoid looking like you can do sleight of hand, as this will scare off the marks in the following hands of poker. But you will come off as an innocent if you start this bit of conjuration with something like "A guy once showed me how to do this trick. I think I remember it. Let me give it a try . . ." And even though I said this trick doesn't suck, it will suck if you try to do it with one of those decks that has pictures of puppy dogs and kitties or flowers on it. You need a real deck of cards that has a white border on the back of the cards. Most decks are like this. Basically, you want that border on the back and not a design that goes all the way to the edge because the edges of the cards need to look the same face-up and face-down. —TR

THE "JUST ONE CARD" ADVANTAGE

Another name for cheating at cards is *advantage play*. Ain't that cute? *Advantage play*. Sounds downright wholesome. If you want to engage in advantage play (and why would you ever want to play fair?), then you have a number of choices. You can spend several years of your life learning how to "move"—which is the covert sleight of hand to manipulate the cards to where they need to be for you to win. It is a tough path to take, but can be financially rewarding—provided that you don't get caught and end up with the nickname Stumpy. Or you can befriend someone that knows how to move and work as a team. Yes, you have to split the money you'll win, but it will be more money than you would have won without your talented cohort. And if you two get caught, there's the chance that they'll beat up your partner first and you'll have an extra moment to find the nearest window. Most partnerships dissolve when one of the partners is pummeled.

But if you don't want to go through all that effort, there is a simple and easy way to achieve your misanthropic goal. It is known as the "just one card" advantage. All you do is remove one card from the deck. It doesn't sound like that would do much to help you, but trust us. If you remove a high card—and we prefer to swallow a court card like a king or queen—it throws the odds heavily in your favor.

You now avoid playing hands that would require that card to make a straight or three of a kind. You know that this card will never be there to help you, but the other lovely folks at the table don't, and that's your advantage. They will be gambling that the card will come up. And it won't. And then you win.

Well, maybe. This little ploy won't win you every hand. But it will put you ahead at the end of the night. You can also remove two cards, but anything more than this will make the deck feel short. Don't put the card (or cards) in your pocket or hide it anywhere on your body. If the card is not on your person, then you can't technically be found guilty of cheating. You still might get your ass kicked, but your assailant will be considered a poor sport, and people will wag their fingers at him. That should teach him a lesson.

BLACK-JACKED!

You have two cards turned over. You tell your mark that the added value of the two cards is twenty-one, and then ask him to guess what the cards are. If he needs a little help, you can give him a hint: One of the cards isn't an ace. If he gives up, reveal that one of the cards isn't an ace . . . but the *other* card is. Revealing the other card with a value of ten takes the total to twenty-one and makes your friend a total fool.

PART 2

Twentieth Century to the Present

LOU BLONGER (1849–1924)

The golden age of grift began at the turn of the century and peaked roughly between 1914 and 1923, a period of unprecedented prosperity for the American upper-middle class. Con men rejoiced: Good fortune can lead to a sense of invincibility and risk taking. The era's slow, haphazard means of communication were also beneficial; for example, it was possible to exploit the interval of time between the end of a horse race and the broadcasting of its results. This was called the Big Store and took on various forms. Blonger built an empire using this type of con, organizing an extensive ring of tricksters that operated in Denver for more than twenty-five years. Central facilities set up to resemble stock exchanges or betting parlors were used alternately by several teams running Big Store cons, convincing suckers to put up large sums of cash in order to secure delivery of promised stock profits or bet winnings.

CHARLES PONZI (1882–1949)

Known as "the man who invented money," Italian-born Ponzi became famous with a breathtaking Peter-to-Paul scam that involved members of Boston's Italian community using postal exchange coupons that were purported to bring a return of ten times the original investment. Ponzi would pay off the first round of investors with money received from later investors. Word spread about the success of the early investors, which ensured a steady stream of people eager to give Ponzi their money to invest. The scenario played out with a collapse of the venture and the loss of millions of dollars. Ponzi has been immortalized by having countless pyramid scams throughout the following decades referred to as "Ponzi schemes."

TITANIC THOMPSON (1892–1974)

No overview of con artists would be complete without dishonorable mention being given to this legendary master miscreant. Born Alvin Clarence Thomas, Thompson came to the attention of the public as a key witness in the 1929 Arnold Rothstein murder trial in New York. Rothstein was the well-heeled gambler and restaurateur who had had a hand in the Chicago "Black Sox" World Series scandal a decade earlier. Thompson and a group of high rollers set up Rothstein in a gambling scam that took him for more than a quarter million dollars. The con went bad and one of the gamblers accidentally shot and killed Rothstein. Thompson and the other gamblers were arrested as suspects, but Titanic soon agreed to be a witness (though not a helpful one; the case was never officially solved). Though he gained notoriety for this event, it was a minor affair compared with some of his efforts in a lifetime of deception. He was the greatest proposition bettor of all time (most of the scams in this book fall under the heading of proposition bets, which are simply bets made on an outcome), and he was also a great athlete who used his physical talents to win bets. (For a list of his sports bets, see page 182.) He even became adept at playing golf in a wheelchair!

"COUNT" VICTOR LUSTIG (1890–1947)
There is not enough space to do justice to the exploits of this amazing man. He sold the Eiffel Tower twice, scammed Al Capone out of five thousand dollars, sold money-making machines to countless people, including law enforcement officers, and made his escape from an "escape-proof" jail (leaving a thank-you note in his cell). And those are just a few highlights of his long career in crime. Many in his industry feel that he was the best there ever was.

SUSANNA MILDRED HILL (*ca.* 1880)
Hill was a con artist who fooled potential suitors. A sixty-year-old mother, she convinced many men that she was a beautiful young woman in her twenties. Hundreds of men sent gifts to their pen pal, victims of a con now known as the Lonely Hearts scam.

FRANK WILLIAM ABAGNALE JR. (1948–)
Abagnale was an impostor who worked under eight identities—including pilot, doctor, lawyer, and teacher—though he used many more to cash checks. He passed bad checks worth over $2.5 million in twenty-six countries. The Steven Spielberg film *Catch Me If You Can* was based on his autobiography. Currently he runs Abagnale and Associates, a financial fraud consultancy company.

CHRISTOPHE THIERRY ROCANCOURT (1967–)
Rocancourt scammed affluent people by masquerading as a member of the Rockefeller family. His first big con was faking the deed to a property he didn't own, then "selling" the property for $14 million. In Los Angeles, he pretended to be a movie producer, boxing champion, and venture capitalist. Rocancourt owned a couple of Ferraris, befriended Jean-Claude Van Damme, married a *Playboy* model, and lived for a time with Mickey Rourke (not that you have to be a professional con artist to fool Mickey Rourke). Currently, he sits in a Vancouver jail cell and claims he has found God.

This is the story of America.
—JACK KEROUAC, *ON THE ROAD*

CHAPTER 5

CONTINENTAL GRIFT

"Con the Road Again . . ."

Have cons, will travel. In a car or on a plane, on a boat or on a train: On the road is the perfect time to be on your marks. For what sucker is better than someone you may never see again? Sure, the legendary con artists made careers of bouncing from town to town, hitting the bricks before marks caught on to the scam, but these days, you might just want a few tricks to help pass the time on yet another boring business trip.

HEAD FOR BUSINESS

Matthew 19:24 says, "It is easier for a camel to go through the eye of a needle than for a rich man to enter the kingdom of God." We say, "Okay, Matty Boy, but can you stick your head through a business card in order to enter a sweeter hotel room? We can."

WHAT IT'S GOOD FOR:
Betting for a hotel room upgrade at the front desk.

WHAT YOU NEED:
- A business card
- Scissors

WHAT YOU DO:

1 It's late at night and you're checking in to a hotel. There's no line at the registration desk and only one clerk on duty. Produce a business card and wager that you can cut a hole in it and stick your head through it.

2 Fold the business card in half, the long way.

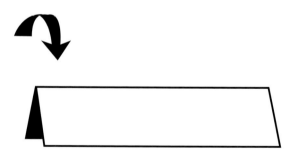

I learned this stunt during the Girl Scouts. Hey, you scout for what you want and I'll scout for what I want. —TR

3 Starting about an eighth of an inch from the end, cut a straight line down from the fold, stopping about an eighth of an inch from the bottom.

4 Moving another eighth of an inch down, cut a straight line up from the bottom, stopping an eighth of an inch from the fold.

5 Move down the card, alternating steps three and four, until you reach the end, with your last cut down from the top.

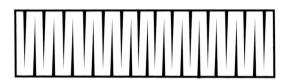

6 Cut along the fold, from the first cut mark to the last (leave both ends intact).

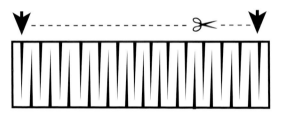

7 Carefully unfold this crazy-looking thing you've created to form a large paper jig-jagged ring that will easily fit over your head.

"TICKET, PLEASE"

True story. Three older con artists were on a train to Chicago, looking to make some easy money before continuing on to Los Angeles. They took a seat across from three young guys who were talking a bit too loudly about some scams they had just pulled in St. Louis. The three young grifters laughed to themselves as they pulled their three tickets out, ready to be collected. This just made the old men snicker, since they only pulled out a single ticket for the three of them. That got the young Turks' attention. "How's that work?" they wondered.

"Watch and learn," the old grifters told them.

When they saw the conductor one car away, the three men piled into the restroom and closed the door. The conductor appeared and, seeing that someone was in the bathroom, knocked on the door. "Ticket, please." The door opened a crack, and one hand poked out to hand the conductor the single ticket. The conductor punched it and continued on. Soon enough the men emerged and shared a laugh with the boys, who admitted, "For a bunch of old geezers, that was pretty good."

A few days later, waiting for the train to L.A., the three old con men bumped into the youngsters on the train platform. The boys nudged the men and held up a single ticket: "It's our turn this time." The men wished them luck and said they didn't even have one ticket. (Chicago was a bust and they were heading out broke.) The boys expressed some unconvincing concern, but the older guys just shrugged. "Don't worry, we'll figure something out."

As the train departed, the young scamsters used the same method they learned on the way up. With the conductor one car away, the three piled into the restroom. Soon after they closed the door behind them, one of the old men quickly walked over, knocked on the door, and said in a deep voice, "Ticket, please . . ."

Anytime someone starts a tale with "true story," it is either a complete lie or a boring anecdote embellished for entertainment purposes. —TR

"GO WEST, YOUNG MAN"

You've got your map out at a gas station and are asking for directions. May as well make this bet with the guy behind the counter. Maybe he'll let you walk away with a free bag of jerky. It's a simple geographical "gotcha" that gets them every time.

Which city is further west:

a Los Angeles, California

b Reno, Nevada

c San Diego, California

d Phoenix, Arizona

The shocking answer? Reno. You'll just have to trust us on this one. If you want longitude information, go buy an atlas.

This is a good example of "a little knowledge can be a dangerous thing" . . . dangerous to others, that is. —TR

THE
AMERICON
WAY

Is New York City the United States' con capital? There are so many historic scam sites in NYC (for goodness sake, the entire island was swindled away for a few colorful beads and a pat on the back) that we've had to set aside an entire section just to cover it (see page 139). But any U.S. con tour would be incomplete without a visit to these places along the way:

COOPERSTOWN, NEW YORK

Yes, there is the ball museum thing there, but we recommend the Farmers' Museum and seeing the final resting place of the Cardiff Giant. This was a glorious and profitable hoax from 1869. A con man "discovered" a huge cementlike sculpture of a human being buried on his farm. He convinced thousands of people that this was actually the remains of a prehistoric race of giants. Though it was discredited shortly after it surfaced, people still paid good money to see it, and they still do today. The idea of this makes our hearts sing.

FARMINGTON, MICHIGAN

P. T. Barnum knew a good thing when he saw one, so of course he created his very own fake Cardiff Giant. This bogus big fella can now be found at Marvin's Marvelous Mechanical Museum.

CAPE FEAR COUNTY, NORTH CAROLINA

Okay, author Guy Owen made up Cape Fear County, but in his novel *The Ballad of the Flim-Flam Man* it existed in eastern North Carolina and was the base of operations for Mordecai Jones, Owen's legendary con artist (later played by George C. Scott in the movie adaptation, *The Flim-Flam Man*). Jones and his partner Curley worked the "Suckerbelt" which spread across the region.

FIFTEENTH STREET, CHEYENNE, WYOMING

It was on this block that a nineteenth-century grifter named Ben Marks got suckers to come to him by opening a store with "valuable merchandise" all priced at a dollar. The patsies would come in for the bargain and Ben would steer them to the back of the store, where the three-shell game was being played. Years later, some grifters discovered that they could make more of a profit selling the one-buck merchandise than fleecing the customers, and this is how a major Chicago department store chain got its start.

EAST ST. LOUIS, ILLINOIS
OVERLAND PARK, KANSAS
GILBERT, ARIZONA
MOLOKAI, HAWAII

Just a small sampling of cities purported to be the birthplace of Todd Robbins.

CHICAGO, ILLINOIS

The Windy City is definitely another contender for the title of Scamville, USA. From entertainment (it's where *The Sting* takes place) to politics (Chi Town gave us the expression "vote early and vote often") to sports (let's not forget that the team that disgraced a sport, the scandalous 1919 White Sox, played their home games in this toddlin' town), there is not a single aspect of the city that has not been associated with some sort of graft and grift. No surprise then that this is also the birthplace of David Mamet, the bard of bunco.

CAMP CHESTERFIELD, CHESTERFIELD, INDIANA

This Spiritualist retreat has been going strong since 1886. It should be noted that many of the greatest grifters of all time, such as Jerry Mugivan and the Harmony Kid, came from Indiana, so it is appropriate that the state should be the home of one of the longest-running sites of dubious religion. You can still find mediums working Camp Chesterfield, but the days of darkroom séances with bells and tambourines floating around and the ghost of your great-aunt Tillie walking among you are long gone. Creating that kind of phenomenon is a bit too risky these days, so the best you will get is Tillie whispering a message into the ear of a medium. It is too bad, because in the old days, Spiritualists sometimes could even bring back a dead loved one for conjugal visits! The spook racket just ain't what it used to be.

(continued)

ST. VINCENT CHARITY HOSPITAL, CLEVELAND, OHIO

Where Jack Lemmon and Walter Matthau hatch their phony paralysis plan in Billy Wilder's fraud classic *The Fortune Cookie.*

CORNER OF SEVENTEENTH & MARKET STREETS, DENVER, COLORADO

Soapy Smith's activities reached all the way to Alaska, but his grifting empire began in Denver. This corner is where he founded the Tivoli Club, his gambling saloon full of gaming activities, shops, and auctions—many of which were rigged to some degree. According to legend, a sign above the door even warned, "Buyer beware" (but in Latin, of course: *caveat emptor*).

HAYS, KANSAS

The shooting location for the highly recommended grifter film *Paper Moon.* Added bonus: Buffalo Bill used to live here.

INVISIBLE COTTON FIELDS, TEXAS

In the late 1950s, financier/weasel Billie Sol Estes received many millions in government subsidies for growing cotton—that did not exist. The scandal-filled following years involved indictments, mysterious deaths, prison time, and Estes's claim that Lyndon Johnson was behind the Kennedy assassination.

HOTEL DEL CORONADO, CORONADO, CALIFORNIA

Located outside San Diego, this hotel houses the ghost of an actual con artist. In the late 1880s, Kate Morgan would lure train passengers into a game of cards with her "brother" Tom (in fact, husband Tom), who would easily scam their money. In 1892, Kate learned she was pregnant and wanted to stop working the trains. Tom didn't. After a fight, Kate checked in to room 302 (now 3312) and waited for her husband to join her for Thanksgiving. When he didn't show, she bought a gun and was found shot in the head on the steps leading down to the beach. There have been sightings of her ghost ever since. Recent theories suggest it was Tom's doing, not suicide.

NICKELED AND DIMED

We believe in traveling light. This coin con only requires a nickel and a dime. And this time they've been provided for you—since you've just nabbed a counter seat at Route 66's Runnin' on Fumes Café and someone just left a fifteen-cent tip for their cup o' joe. There's a nickel half resting on a dime right there on the counter. So before the waitress can clear them away, bet her that you can move the nickel, which is currently on top, *under* the dime without touching the dime. Ask for the breakfast special—on the house, of course—if you can pull this off.

How's it done? Simply take the nickel and hold it under the counter top, below the dime. Make cents? Enjoy the hash browns.

A HANDFUL

The bus has just pulled over at a rest stop, and the loser who's been making loud, obnoxious comments since Delaware is about to open a new pack of cigarettes. Time to shut him up.

There is nothing redeeming about A HANDFUL. It is mean-spirited and will leave your victim bewildered and/or pissed off. There is no reason to do this to anyone . . . unless it's that loser that gets on everyone's nerves or some overbearing jerk. If this person smokes, you owe it to yourself and your fellow travelers to do this jape on him. It will be very therapeutic. —TR

WHAT IT'S GOOD FOR:
Payback. And possibly saving a life.

WHAT YOU NEED:
• A pack of cigarettes

WHAT YOU DO:

1   Challenge the mark to see if he can hold all the cigarettes in the pack between his index and middle fingers—the same fingers in which a smoker usually holds a single smoke—as if he were going to smoke the entire pack at once. Tell him that it may sound easy but is pretty tough . . . you saw someone do it, but it looked almost impossible. In fact, you're willing to give him a dollar if he can do it.

2   If he tries, he'll soon realize that your help is needed—not enough hands to pull out the smokes and place them between his fingers. Offer to hold the pack, making it easier to take out the cigarettes.

3   He'll probably manage to do it successfully. It's not terribly difficult. Now give him the dollar and completely crumple up the cigarette pack, tossing it into the garbage—and walk away. He'll have a handful of cigarettes and no place to put them.

PACKING

One of the differences between you and me is what is in our luggage. We might be standing next to each other at the luggage carousel, and our bags might look identical (and having nondescript luggage can be a useful tool for a con man. A grifter will grab a mark's bag instead of his, and when the chump beefs, the con will apologize and offer to buy him a drink—thus the door is open for all sorts of possibilities). But what is inside is one of the things that sets us apart.

If you opened my bag, you might find:

A SUIT, still in the dry-clean covering. I might be changing my clothes quickly and will not have time to iron or steam my coat. After all, looking sharp is one of the Ten Commandments for Con Men (see page 193). So that plastic keeps it from wrinkling. And I don't care what's printed on dry cleaning wrapping, that plastic bag *does* make a great play toy for a bratty kid.

AN OLD CREDIT CARD. It can be useful for jimmying open a door. I like carrying either someone else's old discarded card or one of the cards credit companies send when they try to entice you to sign your life away to them. It is a fake card that has no name or number on it. Those kinds of cards are great to give to a bartender to run a tab. You have a few rounds, schmooze up the bar staff, become everybody's new best friend, and then step outside to have a smoke, never to be seen again.

A PACK OF MARKED CARDS. I leave those cards sitting around a lobby or waiting area while I am reading my paper. Someone will discover them, and before you know it, a game starts up. I join in reluctantly (I have an appointment to get to soon) and have amazing luck. I pick up my winnings and get the hell out. By the way, I always do this in the lobby of a hotel that I am *not* staying in.

A PAIR OF GLASSES. I like to pick up glasses from thrift shops. I buy ones that have very weak lenses. You can't travel without some sort of disguise, and it is amazing how you can totally change the way you look by combing your hair differently and putting on a pair of glasses. It is a trick I picked up from a guy named Clark Kent.

A SMALL BOTTLE OF "STINK PERFUME." Available in your finer gag and magic shops, this stuff is usually called Morning Breeze or some other soft and gentle name. The reality is this stuff smells like decomposing prenatal chickens, i.e. rotten eggs. When I check in to a hotel, I have the bellhop carry my bags up to the room. I let him go in first, and while he's not looking, I take out the "perfume" and sprinkle some on the carpet. I talk to the bellhop for a moment while looking for some cash. I need to stall a bit to allow the smell to waft forth. I then notice the smell (ofttimes the bellhop notices it first), and the bellhop calls the front desk for another room. It is the damndest thing, but the smell is in that room too. I then call down to the desk and ask what is going on in the hotel. I make a vague reference to Legionnaires' disease and that perhaps the health department should be called. Before you know it, I am moved into a suite.

A SMALL FRAMED PHOTO OF MY SAINTLY MOTHER. It's a lovely shot of her that was taken right after she got out of prison. This photo is the last thing I see as I drift off to sleep. It keeps her in my thoughts and reminds me that she owes me seven hundred bucks. I love you, Ma, but a bet is a bet.

THE **MATCH-UP**

A perfect con when you find yourself at a bar in some airport killing time because your flight has been delayed.

WHAT IT'S GOOD FOR:
Winning a drink to anesthetize yourself as the layover drags on and on.

WHAT YOU NEED:
• A box of matches
• A glass

WHAT YOU DO:

1   Empty the box of matches onto the bar.

2   Turn over a glass and put the matchbox on top so that it hangs off by half an inch.

3   Put your finger under the overhanging part of the matchbox and lift up until the box is standing on its end. That's it: Just slowly lift until it's standing up straight. Take your time; you don't need to flip it up or anything. Gentle, gentle.

4   Stand it up a couple of times. This unusual sight will gain the attention of one of your fellow barflies. Explain that it is harder to do than it looks. (It is.)

5   Move the glass and box over to him and ask him to give it a try. He is able to do it, though he finds it is not as easy as he thought. You say that he had good beginner's luck, and if he can do it again, you will buy him a drink—but if the box falls over, he buys you a drink.

6   Now, when he tries, he fails. The box falls over.

WHAT'S THE SECRET:

The key is how you reset the matchbox for the mark. When you push it up, and when the mark tries it the first time, the matchbox is right side up (see fig. 1). But when you reset it for that second try, you turn it upside down. This means that the inner drawer of the box is upside down (see fig. 2), and the extra weight of the box bottom on the opposite side will throw the balance off and will cause the box to gain a bit more momentum when it is being pushed up and therefore topple over. It just simply will not stop when it becomes vertical. Over it goes.

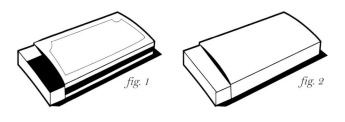

fig. 1

fig. 2

This scam is based on the old carnival game called Bottle Up. It is a simple game of trying to get an empty beer bottle to stand up by slowly lifting it. What most folks don't know is that beer bottles have one side that is heavier and thicker than the other. Set the bottle with the heavy side down and it stands up easily. Set it down with the heavy side up and it will topple over. You can't fight gravity . . . it's the law. —TR

THE
WINNER'S
CIRCLE

When asking how to get back to the highway, you often hear as many different sets of directions as there are people in the room. With this scam, what looks to be the longer distance between two points turns out to be the quickest trip to the winner's circle.

WHAT IT'S GOOD FOR:
Getting a late-night meal during an all-night drive.

WHAT YOU NEED:
• A tall glass
• Assorted items, such as a cell phone, a wallet, a pack of cigarettes, and an ashtray

WHAT YOU DO:
1   You just finished a glass of cola to wash down your burger. Why pay for either? Bet that the circumference of the top of the glass is greater than the height of the glass.

2   The waiter, your mark, might hesitate. While it looks like you might be wrong, it stands to reason you probably know something he doesn't. So make it more interesting. Put the glass on top of a bunch of different objects, adding to the total height—and still maintain that the circumference of the top is greater. The more stuff you put the glass on, the more you can bet.

3   Put the glass on an upside-down ashtray.

4   Need more? Put it on a cell phone. A wallet. Keep going, and keep betting. If you feel like you've already won dinner, go for dessert.

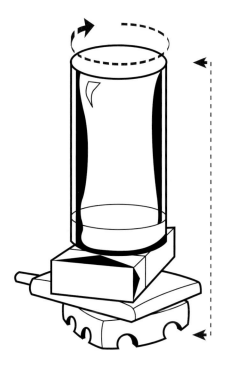

5 When you're out of things or the tower is surely going to topple soon, use an unfolded napkin to help with the measurements. First wrap it around the top to get the circumference (make a mark where it begins to overlap) and then drop it down the side of the cup to show the difference.

6 So what if the cola residue shorted out your cell phone? You just ate a free burger!

This is an impossible-looking bet. Simply put, it works with almost any glass or mug, and if he takes the bet, and he will, the mark will lose. The beauty of this ploy is that you don't have to do anything. It's just a freakish thing and works automatically. Go ahead and measure the circumference of any cup, glass, or mug you have near you. Now measure its height. See? I wouldn't fool you for nothing. I'd fool you for something, but not for nothing. —TR

HALF
A CHANCE

You're in a train station waiting to board, just reading the morning paper. So's the guy next to you. *Perfect.* Wager a donut to-go on whether or not he can fold a page from the paper in half more than seven times . . . that is, take a full sheet and fold it in half, then in half again, and again, and so on—eight times. See if he'll take you up on it. If he does, you'll see him lose. The chances of doing this are zero . . . a big ol' donut.

And there is a rehash on this stunt. After the mark has lost the bet, bet him that you can fold your newspaper in half twelve times. Make the bet double or nothing. In order for the mark to take the bait, make it seem like something you might not be able to do. Play a note of uncertainty in your voice. When the schnook goes for it, fold the paper in half, then open it up and fold it in half again, then open it up and fold it in half again, etc. You could do this all day, which is a good thing as you will need that exercise to work off the calories from all those donuts. —TR

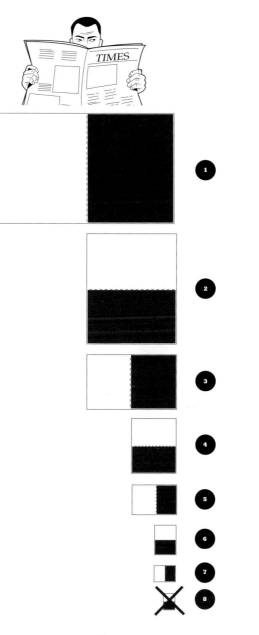

CROSS-COUNTRY CONS

Ever thought you had planned a "cheap" trip and ended up paying it off for the rest of the year? The travel industry is aiming to soak you, make no mistake about it. But there are always a few ways for the modern con man to fight back when on the road. You'll end up with some extra bucks for the important things: poker, booze, and women.

 **BEGINNER**

FOR CUSTOMERS ONLY?
Keep cups from coffee chains, and the next time you pass another café in the chain, get the matching cup out of your trunk and simply appear to be a recent customer. This will allow you to hang out, mingle, use the bathroom, read the paper, get water—all essentials to a guy on the road—for no cost.

GUESS WHO'S CONNING TO DINNER
When you travel, always look for a meeting of Episcopalians. They do throw some wonderful family-style meals where all, even travelers just passing through, are welcome. And if anybody tries to spew any religious mumbo jumbo your way, take sick pride in the fact that you're probably sinning just by being there.

 **INTERMEDIATE**

GAS ATTACK

After takeoff, discreetly let the flight attendant know that the person next to you can't stop farting. It can't be any other complaint, and you have to say "farting." The whole situation will be so awkward that you might be able to have your pick of other seat options and, depending on the flight, maybe even an upgrade.

INSTANT CELEBRITY

The day before you check in to a hotel, call pretending to be from different press outlets asking if you've arrived. "Hello, I'm calling from the *Beavertown Gazette* . . . has author Joe Blow checked in yet?" "Hi, I'm sure you're not going to tell me, but my editor at the *Spring Oaks Journal* wants me to see if Joe Blow is staying at your hotel this evening . . ." You might be able to ask for certain favors or be granted special treatment when you finally do check in. Hell, be a sport and sign an autograph or two. You haven't let fame get to your head, have you?

⬤ ⬤ ⬤ ◯ **PRO**

PUT THIS ONE OVER—EASY!

You enter a diner, sit at the counter, and order a cup of coffee. A few minutes later, your partner takes a seat next to you, though you two never talk. He orders a full breakfast and enjoys it. You ask for your checks at about the same time. This scam only works in restaurants where you can pay up front or at the counter, because your partner takes *your* bill, pays up front, and leaves. Soon after, you realize that you got the wrong bill and say that you're not paying for a full breakfast. Pay for your coffee and split. Rendezvous with your partner and head up the road so that you can now get *your* breakfast.

OOPS, I MADE A MIRACLE

Prestain a napkin with some coffee, painting a loose rendering of the region's religious savior of choice. When you're stopping in a small town's roadside diner, spill your coffee, swap out your "miracle napkin," and receive free meals, press, love, and adoration. Couldn't be easier.

(continued)

 **MASTER**

THE CHANGE RAISER

This one's way complicated, takes a long time to perfect, and—while hugely popular with a certain type of con man—is quite risky. Besides needing to have the routine down cold, you need to find a very hurried cashier at the gas station quickmart to make it work. In fact, having an accomplice posing as an impatient stranger behind you can really help.

1   You buy a small item at the counter for fifty cents, but say you only have a ten-dollar bill on you. Apologize and use it to pay, getting your $9.50 in change before turning to go.

2   Before the next person can get to the counter, you suddenly realize you had fifty cents in your pocket all along and turn back, showing the worker and wondering aloud if you can give back the change he gave you for the original ten dollars.

3   You place the $9.50 on the counter and take the ten-dollar bill back, when you obviously realize that you still owe the fifty cents that you found in your pocket.

4   So you slide over the fifty cents to the $9.50 still sitting there, and then drop the ten you just took back on top and say, "It might be easier if you could just take all this change and give me a twenty. Thanks so much."

5   When the cashier adds the amount on the counter, it does add up to twenty. If the pressure is on and he's not paying attention, once he hands you a twenty, he won't realize you just doubled your money.

THE LAYOVER CONTINUES

You don't *want* to keep drinking. But the more they delay your flight, the longer you have to sit at the overpriced terminal bar and grill and do *something*. Same with the guy next to you. (But you don't want to pull that matchbox stunt again.) So here's a little challenge to keep you up for a little longer, and maybe win you some refreshments in the meantime. Take out a business card and fold the two diagonally opposite corners over just a little, then lay the card down on the bar with the bent corners down. Now make a bet that the guy can't blow under the card so that it flips over and lands on its back. Try as he might, it won't happen.

When it's your turn, carefully blow it over to the edge of the bar so that half is hanging off, then blow up from underneath and watch it flip right over.

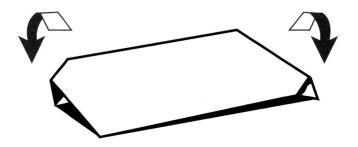

IMITATION
IS THE SINCEREST FORM OF THIEVERY

Everywhere you go in this great land of ours, you will notice that people talk funny. Keep your ears open and you will notice a number of regional verbal peccadilloes. For instance, if you hear someone pronounce a word like *idea* as *idear* and a word like *runner* as *runna*, then chances are they are from the Boston area (or *arear*). And there is no mistaking that flat *a* sound of the folks from Chic-*ah*-go. If you run into a person with a Southern way of speaking that also has touches of Brooklyn in their speech, they be from N'awlins. People that like use like the word *like* like a lot and like end every sentence like it is like a question are like from like the West Coast.

Catalog these provincial variations, and when you hear them, ask if the person is from that part of the country. This is a great way to start a conversation, but only if the person is not in their hometown. Noticing that someone is speaking with a Memphis dialect when you are in Memphis and then asking that person if they are from Memphis will only show off that you are from Dorkville.

The next step in this process is to learn to mimic those ways of speaking. If you subtly sneak them into your speech when you are speaking with someone from that region, it will give them a sense of familiarity and make them feel comfortable . . . and then you can hurt them. Are we speaking your language?

NEW YORK

IF YOU CAN TAKE IT THERE, YOU CAN TAKE IT ANYWHERE . . .

Remember what the snake used to trick Eve? Well, it's no coincidence that this town's also known as the Big Apple.* From the Coney Island of yesteryear, where three-card monte was played openly on the beach back in the 1880s, to Canal Street, where today they're still taking suckers' money with the same game, it's clear that grift has always been alive in New York.

---

* It's also known as Gotham, a nickname with an interesting history. The word literally means "goat town," and the original Gotham is a small city in Nottinghamshire, England, which was regarded as a village of idiots back in the Middle Ages. However, many believed that the residents only pretended to be fools in order to con others and avoid the maintenance costs of the king. In 1807, Washington Irving used the name in a pointed remark toward New Yorkers and their own brand of simpleminded cleverness . . . and somehow the name stuck.

THE BROOKLYN BRIDGE

George Parker (1870–1936) was one of the most ballsy grifters ever, selling quite a few city landmarks to gullible tourists. He sold the Brooklyn Bridge on an average of twice a week for years, and it was not unusual for buyers to begin construction of their own tollbooths before police broke the news to them. Since Parker, the perfect marks are described as "gullible enough to buy the Brooklyn Bridge."

THE BROOKLYN BRIDGE

This bridge is just way too grand for one one flimflam footnote. On July 23, 1886, Steve Brodie became famous after jumping off the bridge—and surviving—which created publicity for a bar that he soon opened. It also inspired the phrase "pull a Brodie," which means doing something dangerous. All this despite the fact that the jump was likely a hoax.

THE OYSTER BAR, BASEMENT OF GRAND CENTRAL STATION, FORTY-SECOND STREET AND PARK AVENUE

Rumored to be a well-established meeting spot for con artists for generations. But you didn't hear it from us.

CORNER OF FORTY-SEVENTH STREET AND BROADWAY

Former location of Ames Billiard Hall, where Fast Eddie Felson and Minnesota Fats face off at the end of *The Hustler*.

CANAL STREET

Knockoff goods are one of the few areas where the marks are in on the con. People generally know that a Rolex watch doesn't cost eight bucks, that the handbag brand isn't spelled "Kate Spayed," and that the Louis Vuitton pattern doesn't have a little icon of two midgets playing patty-cake in it. But nobody cares. Tourists come to New York specifically to buy this crap. It looks close enough to the real thing, the quality is acceptable, and hey, it's a bargain. So don't ask, don't tell—and don't let that "leather" come in contact with your skin for more than forty minutes at a stretch.

WALL STREET

Where to begin with this one? We considered starting with the idea of "short selling," but maybe it's just best to get back to this in one of our later volumes, *The Modern Con Man's Guide to Financial Investments.*

254 WEST FIFTY-FOURTH STREET

At this address stood the legendary Studio 54 club, where in 1983, David Hampton first pretended to be the son of actor Sidney Poitier. Hampton, employing the "they-think-we-all-look-alike" ploy, gained entry to the club, and in the months to come, duped celebs and society folk into giving him meals, lodging, and money. His exploits inspired a play, a movie, and a prison term.

GRANT'S TOMB, RIVERSIDE DRIVE AND 122ND STREET

George Parker sold this, too, posing as Grant's grandson.

91 NASSAU STREET,
FORMER ADDRESS OF THE *NEW YORK SUN*

The *Sun* became famous when it published a series of articles in 1835 reporting sightings—through new advanced telescopes—of life on the moon. The stories, printed as fact, described unicorns and winged humanoids that lived amidst trees and beaches. When these fictional news stories upped the circulation, an important and exciting journalistic trend was started.

MADISON SQUARE GARDEN,
SEVENTH AVENUE AND THIRTY-SECOND STREET

Also sold by George Parker. He prepared like hell for these sales, going so far as to set up phony offices and fake documents to prove his "legal ownership."

METROPOLITAN MUSEUM OF ART,
FIFTH AVENUE AND EIGHTY-SECOND STREET

Yep, also sold by Parker.

STATUE OF LIBERTY

You-know-who did you-know-what.

CHAPTER 6

SCAMS IN LOVE

Cupid Cons and Other Ways to Avoid a Valentine's Day Massacre

Love: Some say it's the biggest con of all. Maybe that's too cynical for the modern con man, but there are still plenty of scams to pull in the world of dating and relationships. After all, throughout history, love has been associated with more games, tricks, deceptions, and misdeeds than any other human endeavor. Why come to the party empty-handed?

---

* Trivia: Lead vocals by Cuba Gooding Sr.

HEADS OVER HEELS

We've all flipped for a girl. In this trick, your girl "flips" for you.

WHAT IT'S GOOD FOR:
Bonding with a date—you're accomplices now.

WHAT YOU NEED:
- A coin
- A flat surface

WHAT YOU DO:

1   Bet someone that, even with your eyes closed, you can tell if a flipped coin lands heads or tails just by listening to it. To prove that it's not a lucky guess, you can do it ten times in a row.

2   To make sure it's fair—we are constantly stressing fairness in this book, aren't we?—a third party will flip the coin and verify if the guesses are right. The third party happens to be your date.

3   Prior to making the bet, you've set up a code with your date. (Oh well, so much for fairness.) The code is established after the first flip. If the coin lands on heads, your date says something. Anything. ("What is it?" or "Okay" or "Move over, I can't see the coin" or "My god you're gorgeous." Maybe that last one is too suspicious.) If it's tails, your date says nothing.

4   You amazingly guess correctly.

5   On the *next* flip, the code is *reversed*: Heads she says nothing; tails she says something.

6   For each successive flip, the code alternates back and forth: heads something, heads nothing. And so on.

WHAT IF YOU FORGET WHERE YOU ARE?
The longer you're flipping, or the more you've had to drink before beginning this bet, the likelier it is that one of you will lose your place at some point. So it's important to have a code reset. If you or your date ever says "Wait," the code reverts to the original setup: Heads, say something; tails, say nothing.

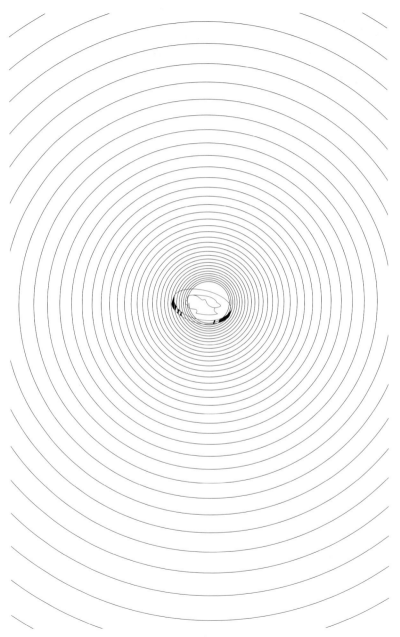

BEWARE MISS GRIFT

Feel bad about scamming the so-called weaker sex? Don't. As a modern con man, it stands to reason that you'll go on a date or two with the modern con *woman*. In songs she's been known as Devil in a Blue Dress, Black Magic Woman, Evil Woman, Devil Woman, Witchy Woman, and a thousand other names. But to us, she is simply Miss Grift. The fact is, she has a few tricks up her sleeves, even in a sleeveless dress. Here are a few of her female flimflams to look out for. And be careful . . . she's worked these for years and has them down cold.

"DISTRESS CALL" DECEPTION

This sinister and sly move, originating in Chicago, has Miss Grift's cell phone ringing during a rendezvous for drinks with you, her mark. Whoops, sorry, she has to take it. "Hmm. Oh yeah? Where are you? Okay, okay." She feels bad but her friend is depressed and needs her help, and she has to split. Oh, but don't be fooled—that was really her accomplice, and the conversation was scripted. The bottom line is she's bored and bailing.

HOW TO COUNTERACT: Have the date in some basement club with little to no reception. Or, early in the evening, make a big show of turning off your phone so the two of you won't be disturbed. She'll either follow suit or look like an ass when the call does come in.

THE LEAVE IT TO CLEAVAGE*

This con first swept the coasts over twenty years ago and has been Miss Grift's hallmark ever since, because if there's one thing she knows, it's that we're all crazy for cleavage. It's one of the Seven Wonders of the World. Maybe even two of them. But try not to be hypnotized. Many a girl has weaseled a date out of a low-cut top. And many times, it's not even real. Cleavage can be the creation of high-tech undergarments, tape, straps, hooks, belts, pulleys, flying buttresses, and witchcraft. Get that top off and you'll be confronted with something flatter than the Mojave.

HOW TO COUNTERACT: Her eyes are up here, guys.

THE COVER GIRL CON

In a similar vein as Leave It to Cleavage is this classic "date and switch" routine, which guarantees Miss Grift will always look her best on date numero uno. She'll get her hair blown out, dress to the nines, and even stop by Bergdorff's for a professional makeover. She might even suggest a bar with low lighting. Do not be taken by this classic con.

HOW TO COUNTERACT: Playfully tell her you don't believe she's old enough to drink and that you need to check her age on her driver's license. Then look at the picture. That's what you'll be dating in two months.

SUPPERTIME SCAM

For three years in the late nineties, Miss Grift crisscrossed the country surviving exclusively on this no-good grift. If you were unfortunate enough to fall victim to it, you know how it ends. She was not attracted to you, she would not sleep with you, and you were nothing but a credit card that night, until after dinner, when, oh, she suddenly grew so tired! (Miss Grift practices her yawn as much as her deadly smile.) She spun some yarn about having to wake up early the next day. A quick thanks for din-din and this bird was bye-bye—until she got hungry again.

HOW TO COUNTERACT: Do not have dinner on the first three dates.

(continued)

---

* This reminds us of another scam of hers from the seventeenth and eighteenth centuries called Wolf in the Breast—and this is 100 percent real! The Miss Grift of that era would go up to a mark on the street with her chest sticking out, heaving in his direction, cleavage all but spilling over, crying out in pain. She would then ask for money to get some medical attention for her current ailment, which happened to be having a wolf trapped within her and gnawing at her breasts from inside. It's as wonderfully silly as it is evil, for who among us would be able to turn away and not help? Miss Grift, she gets us every time!

DATING DECOY

Miss Grift has no shame. With this truly diabolical move, she keeps marks like you running in circles while she builds up a steady dating pool of other no-chancers with the sole purpose of using your collective attention to entice her real interest. After all, if she is so in demand, she must be worth something. You were a pawn, and this queen planned to sacrifice you from the start.

HOW TO COUNTERACT: Load up your social-networking site's friend list with as many hot ladies as possible. She'll check there, because they always do, and, oh my, he's quite a player himself!

THE SWITCHEROOMMATE SCAM

This originated in nineteenth-century Europe and migrated to our shores soon after, where it has continued to thrive ever since. In it, Miss Grift continues to come over to hang out at your pad, only to let it drop two weeks later that she's totally into your roommate. All along you were trying to get her into your bed, and she's been more interested in the room across the hall. Gee, that would've been nice to know before the dinners, the movies, the walks, and the poetry.

HOW TO COUNTERACT: Be a stand-up guy. Wish the dame luck and put in a good word to your roommate. Just please make sure he knows about her ample back hair.

MISTER RIGHT IS WRONG

Sometimes as a guy, it's hard to admit you're wrong. And not being able to admit it can lead to some pretty rough times. But here's a very simple little bet in which you'll be thrilled to be incorrect. Say you're sitting on a park bench and you just met a cute little lady next to you. Pull out three coins so that she sees them clearly and close your fist around them. Ask her, "Would you believe I now have *four* coins in my hand? Seriously. Would you at least agree to let me buy you a drink if I'm wrong?" If she agrees, show that you still only have three coins. You *were* wrong. And, if you didn't screw up the wording of the wager, it's time for those drinks.

CAN'T LET GO • Nervous to take her hand for the first time? Don't be. Here's a simple bet to make on a first date—because in order to position her hands properly, there's gonna have to be some touchin'. And that might just ignite the spark you've been waiting for.

Place her two hands together, palms touching. (Curb any temptation to whisper, "Your prayer has been answered already . . . here I am.") Next, bend her middle fingers over so they rest on the knuckle of the opposite hand.

Now just place a coin between her two touching ring fingers (see fig. 1) and see if she can separate them enough to drop the coin onto the table. She won't be able to.

Oops, you were so excited to touch real female flesh you forgot to actually wager anything. Now that she's lost, go double or nothing with a related bet . . .

IT'S A SNAP • Slide a match between her ring, middle, and index fingers (see fig. 2) and bet that she won't be able to break the match. Her fingers and arm need to remain straight out. If she can't do it, show her how (and win the bet): Keep everything straight and just hit your palm against the table. You he-man, you.

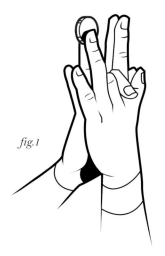

fig.1

CAN'T LET GO

IT'S A SNAP

fig. 2

THE CALLING CARD CON

Talk about a win-win: This next scam lets you win a bet *and* score all sorts of points with your girlfriend. Why? You're encouraging her to tell people how strong your relationship is, and she gets to pursue a favorite hobby: talking on the phone!

WHAT IT'S GOOD FOR:
Showing up a boring couple when you're on a double date.

WHAT YOU NEED:
- A deck of cards
- A cell phone

WHAT YOU DO:

1 You're with another couple. The con goes into effect when you excuse yourself from the group—men's room, jukebox, round of drinks, change in the meter.

2 As soon as you're gone, your girl starts gushing about your relationship. She's never had this sort of bond with anyone. It's like you can read each other's minds. In fact, she can prove it.

3 The girl produces a deck of cards. (What modern con woman doesn't always have a deck of cards with her?) She bets the couple that if they pick a card, any card, and show it to her, that she can call you on the phone and you will correctly guess the card.

4 After your girl has seen the card, she places the call to you and says, "I'm thinking of a card that [friend's name] chose."

5 Since she's the only one who can hear your voice, you can clearly—and slowly—say, "Hearts. Clubs. Diamonds. Spades."

6 As soon as you've said the correct suit, your girlfriend should cut you off, saying, "I'm sending you a mental image of the card."

7 Now you clearly, slowly say, "Two. Three. Four. Five. Six. Seven. Eight. Nine. Ten. Jack. Queen. King. Ace."

8 As soon as you've said the correct number or face card, she should cut you off again. "Have you received the image? I'm putting [friend's name] on the line."

9 You magically say the correct card to him.

10 If you want to try this with a girl you just met, congrats. You've just exchanged phone numbers.

HOW TO SURVIVE A CARNIVAL
and not look like a chump in front of the girl

So it's Friday night and you want to show your sweetie a good time by taking her out to a carnival, county fair, or rinky-dink amusement park. Fine. Enjoy the rides, but be careful around the games. Carnival games will eat you up and spit you out. A date should never end with you flat broke and feeling like a loser. That is what marriage is for.

But there must be a way to win one of those big stupid stuffed animals for your honey, right?

First off, who really wants a four-foot bright purple dog? But for the sake of this discussion, we will assume that possessing one of these useless things is what your beloved desires most (and winning one will ensure your winning something else later on in the evening). So go ahead and try, but just know that most of these games are not there for you to win. We know, shocking. But it's not just that they're hard or even harder than you think, it's that they're rigged. You know about the dull darts that you're throwing at underinflated balloons? What about the bottle toss, where you're trying to knock over a pyramid of three bottles? They each have different weights— with one of the bottom ones weighing anywhere between five and, at one unnamed fair, twenty-eight pounds. (Of course, when the carny demonstrates, the heaviest one is on top, and they all tumble down so nicely.)

There are too many tips and warnings to mention, but one way to win is to slip the carny running the game a twenty-dollar bill when your date ain't looking. Then play the game, win, and claim your prize. (We are referring to the stuffed animal.)*

Actually, the best thing you can do is play a hanky-pank. It sounds dirty and illicit, but it is not. A hanky-pank is a carnival game where you play against other players and someone is guaranteed to win a prize. A good example of a hanky-pank is the water race game where you squirt water into a plastic clown's mouth and the first player that "drowns the clown" wins. (We have found that squirting water into a real clown's mouth until he drowns is more fun, and of benefit to society, but that's another story.) Someone is going to win, and it might be you or your girl.

---

* Bribing a carny to win a game never works. We just put it in there hoping that you won't read this far and will actually try it. We have many carny friends, and putting things like this in the book will make them happy.

CHOPSTICKS

Here's a flirty game to help go from the dining
room to the sake bar, before heading . . . elsewhere.

WHAT IT'S GOOD FOR:
Getting a smile. Value: priceless.

WHAT YOU NEED:
• Chopsticks

WHAT YOU DO:

1   Put your chopsticks in your date's left hand and a twenty-dollar bill in her right.

2   Tell her it's a game in which you're going to ask a bunch of questions, and all she has to do is answer "Chopsticks" to each one. If she does, she wins the twenty. If she answers anything else, she gets your chopsticks and that's it.

YOU: "Got it?"
HER: "Yep."

And so she loses.

3   If she says "Chopsticks," though, you move on, tell her she's quick, and try and trip her up with a seemingly nonquestion follow-up, like "Very good, ready for the next one?"

4   Or you can be playful, by throwing in some questions like "In the summer when you wear a skirt, your legs look like . . . ?" ("Chopsticks.")

5   When you get to the point when she's not saying anything but "Chopsticks":

YOU: "Okay, one last question. Would you rather have the money or the chopsticks?"

Either way, you get your twenty back, which we suggest you offer to use for another round of drinks.

LOVE
&
LARCENY

Yeah, I know, you expect me to give you some advice on how to scam your way to love. Nope. This is one area where—you don't know how much it pains me to write this—being honest is the way to go.

Now, if you are looking to just play Ten Toes, then scam away.* Lying your way through a liaison that has a limited shelf life is very much the way to go. Telling your short-term lover a good fake story about yourself is vital. It will give her something to think about as you are going at it, and it might even distract her from noticing how truly inadequate you are in the sack.

But love is a long-distance journey, and you better be prepared for it. If you are reading this book, then chances are that you are not experienced enough to navigate the deep waters of love using deception as a paddle. You will only find yourself washing up on the rocks of heartbreak. (Man, that was poetic!)

No, my friends, my advice is to make the best hand you can with the cards dealt you, lay them down, and go all in. No bluffing needed. Just let it ride on what you got. You will end up a winner . . . or you won't. And if you lose, pick up your cards and find another table to play at. Somewhere you will find a game where your little pair of threes is a winning combination. (There I go being poetic again.)

---

* This comes from a classic poem:

> There is a game they call Ten Toes,
> It's played all over town,
> The girlies play it ten toes up,
> The guy with ten toes down.

(That was written by William Shakespeare or Maya Angelou. I can't remember which.)

Sometimes, things don't end so well. So if there's an ex that did you wrong, don't bother prank calling her. These days, with caller ID, it's just not worth the headache or the amount of quarters required for a successful pay phone campaign. The best way to get the same results with just a fraction of the effort is to have others do the calling for you—unwittingly. The answer is your office fax machine. You know those preset numbers for popular vendors that have been programmed into it? Well, reset those presets to call Ms. Whatsherface. (Also works on Mr. Whatshisname, the guy she left you for.)

CON-LINE DATING

In the catalog-shopping mentality of online dating, getting noticed is half the battle. Unfortunately—but not unexpectedly—the tall, handsome, successful jerks get noticed a lot more than you. But now's your turn to be a tall, handsome, successful jerk in this game of bait and cyberswitch.

Begin by creating a bogus alternate profile on an online dating site. It's easy enough to obtain a JPEG of some ruggedly handsome dude by Googling "male models." (Just don't do this in front of coworkers. They already think you're weird enough.) Then use your imagination to create an irresistible guy. He's at least six feet two. He's a lawyer or maybe a doctor. He loves animals. Stays fit. Is close to his family. Loves to go out on the town but is just as happy to snuggle on the couch with a bowl of popcorn in front of a DVD, or stay in bed on a lazy Sunday. And he wants to have kids.

Start contacting women you'd like to go out with. Hell, they'll probably start contacting you. E-mail back and forth a few times. Be smooth—you're playing a role. Before typing a sentence, ask yourself, "What would Clooney say?" Don't worry about overly specific questions she asks about your profession, extreme sports hobbies, quaint hometown, etc.—the answers are probably on Wikipedia.

Now, just when it seems like you'd be asking her on a date, you wait an extra couple of days. Then you write to her. "It's hard to say this because I really like you. You're such a great girl. But things have suddenly gotten more serious with someone else, and I don't want to hurt anyone. Hey, this is a crazy idea, but I have a good friend on here—he's a great guy—and I think the two of you might really get along. Here's his profile [it's your real profile!]; check it out and I'll sing your praises to him."

At the very, very least, she'll look at your profile (and see what a charming, cool dude you are), and if you did a good job as the fake dude, she'll probably even go out with you. At which point you're on your own. Though Botox, lifts in your shoes, anabolic steroids, and a small-business loan for some quick cash can all come in handy.

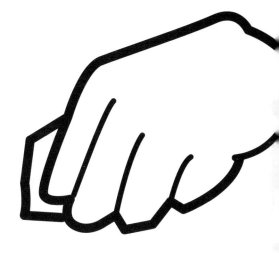

A REAL CONNECTION

You meet a girl. You feel a connection with her. You tell her about this feeling and want to prove it. So you take a dime and put both your hands behind your back. Then bring them out, holding closed fists in front. Now ask her to pick the hand with the dime. She picks one—and is correct! You do it again. Hands behind, then back out in front. Again she picks one. And again she is correct. And then when you go for a third try, she picks the right hand yet again! You *are* psychically linked! You are so totally meant for each other!

   Well, it's either that or the fact that you had a dime in each hand.

IF YOU SEE AN OPENING, TAKE IT

Of all the wonderful cheap date options, perhaps there is none greater than the gallery art opening.*

Right off the bat, you're going to seem oh-so-classy—for an art opening is way cooler than going to the museum, which is the sort of thing you once did on class trips and family vacations. Galleries are about the now, about what's happening today. Man, you are so hip with it! Ahead of the curve!

Now that we got that out of the way, time to bring up the free drinks. A choice of wine, red or white, and as much as you want.

And did someone say "cheese cubes"? Well they should have, because there they are. Sometimes even with jalapeño sprinkles inside. You know how many cheese cubes it takes to get full? Time to find out.

Already tired of talking to your date? Just claim you want to "take in" the paintings. Stand close, stand back, walk around, look at some slides. Take your time and seem deep.

And how about another glass of wine?

Mingle! It's never too late to meet someone else.

If you're actually having fun with your girl, an art gallery is also the

---

* This is also a wonderful travel tip. Art openings are always listed in those weekly city papers. Pick up a copy (often free!) in whatever city you're passing through and plan your evening art crawl—food and drink included.

perfect place to play. Since the biggest collectors are often the ones with the most-torn jeans, no one's going to doubt your interest in buying. Inquire about cost and pretend one of the pieces might look best in the living room. Gallery owners will whisk you into the back, whip up a special drink, and shower you with attention.**

Afterward, step outside and realize that galleries tend to be in more interesting parts of town. Suggest you take a walk together (walks tend to be cost free) and talk about which pieces you like more . . . just make sure you're heading toward the next gallery. Galleries often have openings the same night (check the weekly listings).

** Okay, we lied about this too. Wealth knows wealth. It's like gaydar, but for stock portfolios. Your torn jeans look ratty, theirs look fabulous.

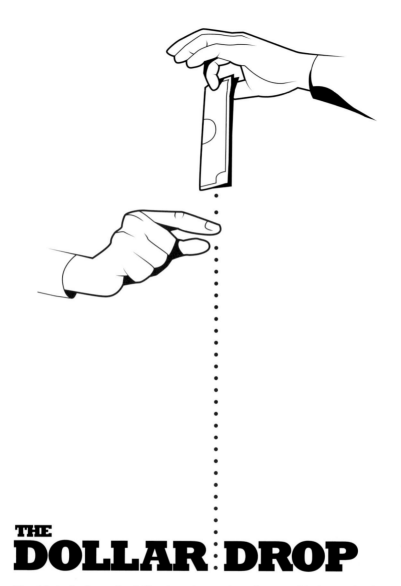

THE
DOLLAR : DROP

No, this isn't about the dollar dropping against the euro. It's just a simple scam to make a girl look good. And if she already looks good—all the better.

WHAT IT'S GOOD FOR:
Wooing a girl away from some loser she's just met.

WHAT YOU NEED:
• A dollar

WHAT YOU DO:
1 Challenge them to a simple test of skill: You will hold a dollar, pinching it with your index finger and thumb, above one of their open hands. You will drop the dollar. The person must snap close their hand, catching the dollar in midair.

2 Let the guy try first. He will fail. Let him try again. He'll fail again.

3 Now it's the girl's turn. Miraculously, she will succeed. Let her try again. She will succeed again.

WHAT'S THE SECRET:
Here's the only difference: With the guy, you're just opening your fingers and letting it go. But when you're dropping the dollar for the girl, lower your hand for a split second before releasing, so you're actually holding on to the dollar for a moment longer. It is as if you are guiding the dollar into her hand, and that extra split second is all it takes for her brain to catch up with her eyes. She should catch it every time.

MORE
-LINE
DATING

If you're instant messaging with a girl, here's a bit of mental manipulation that's a fun way to prove with absolute 100 percent certainty that you two have a strong mental (and perhaps—soon—physical) connection. You're going to read her mind, *over the computer.* Here's an IM transcript of how it should play out.

YOU: Think of a number
    between 1 & 10
HER: Okay
YOU: Multiply it by 9
YOU: Still there?
HER: Yes
YOU: Take ur time
YOU: Still there?
HER: Yes. Okay. Ready
YOU: Did u end up with a
    2-digit number?
HER: Yes
YOU: Add those 2 numbers
    together
YOU: Whenever ur ready
YOU: Just let me know when
HER: Okay ready
YOU: Subtract 5 from that number
HER: Okay
YOU: Go thru the alphabet til
    you get to the letter that
    corresponds with your new
    number. Like if your number
    was 1, it would be A, and
    if it was 2, you'd have B
HER: One minute
YOU: Now think of a country that
    begins with that letter
HER: Okay
YOU: Now take the second letter
    from the country's name and
    quickly think of an animal
    that begins with that letter
HER: Okay
YOU: Something's not right

HER: What?
YOU: I think u screwed this up
HER: Why?
YOU: I don't think there are
    elephants in Denmark.
    Hold on, let me Google . . .

Note: If by some chance she didn't pick Denmark and elephant, hold on to this girl. She's a creative thinker and a keeper. Or else she's totally insane.

AND EVEN MORE CON-LINE DATING

We'd be remiss not to mention one final aspect of con-line dating where you, dear reader, may end up the fool. So be warned, there is a modern-day update of the Lonely Hearts scam that Susanna Mildred Hill perfected. (See Grifter History Part 2 on page 113.) Here's how you can know if you are about to be suckered: If she's hot, foreign, and says she really likes your online profile (*and* thinks you're cute), this may be the beginning of a hot, long e-mail exchange that will end with your wiring money to help her buy a ticket to visit you. Again, the tip-off is she's hot and she's into you. The easiest rule to live by in order to avoid similar cons is, whenever paying for sex, make sure the transaction is face-to-face.

Serious sport has nothing to do with fair play.
—GEORGE ORWELL

CHAPTER 7

SPORT SCAMS

Ways to Grift at Game Time

In sports, it's not how you play the game. It's whether you win. But all that stretching, running, sweating—who needs the aggravation? So whether you're on a team, watching the game at home, or standing in the stadium concession line, there's always a way to come out ahead with these extra tricks for your arsenal. And remember, don't listen to the dissenters: Only losers will use the term *cheating*.

FOOTING THE BILL

Whether a receiver drops a Hail Mary, a runner is tagged out at third, or a layup gets blocked, there's always some blowhard in the room yelling about how much better he could do. So here's a simple bet to point out the mark's own physical limitations.

WHAT IT'S GOOD FOR:
Getting out of paying for the pizza delivery at halftime.

WHAT YOU NEED:
• The pizza delivery bill

WHAT YOU DO:

1 Make a wager: If you lose, the pizza and wings are on you. But if you win, you not only get to just sit back and eat for free—you get the last slice.

2 Explain that you will put the bill on top of the mark's shoe, and he won't be able to bend over and pick it up and hold it out for you to take. If he can do that without moving his feet or falling over, you'll take the bill from him and pay. You can even promise that no one will interfere as he does it.

3 Once he agrees, place him with his back to the wall and heels touching the baseboard.

4 Place the bill on his shoe and ask him to bend over and take it.

5 He won't be able to . . . but he will "pick up" the tab.

REGIONAL RULES

No game of pool is complete without some pissy little argument about the rules. ("I'm just sayin'—where I'm from, you only have to call your shot on a combination. But if that's how you play . . .") You've heard something like it a million times, right? And how many of these "regulations" are straight out of the Pulled-from-Your-Ass Rulebook? Well, these fictional guidelines can come in handy in any competitive situation, and the easiest mark is someone from out of town. ("Hey, you're not from here. That's how we roll in Philly, my friend.") And how are they supposed to argue? Here are some bogus rules to get you started.

- Pool: If you don't hit one of your balls, the cue has to hit all four rails, or you scratch. That's because there used to be four railroad stations around these parts.

- Darts: If someone calls "bullshit" immediately after a bull's-eye, no points are awarded.

- HORSE: You need to make the final shot (E) twice in a row to win.

- Two-Hand Touch: We play three-hand touch.

- Ultimate: After a score, chuck the Frisbee as far as possible, explaining that the visiting team needs to "fetch" after each score.

- Pinball: Visiting opponents must play one-handed when they get multiball. No one knows why.

- Golf: If you hit it into the sand, it's an automatic "do-over," named after local golfing legend Michael Doover.

- Ping-Pong: No, no, we play to twenty-three around here, not twenty-one.

- Arm Wrestling: When you're a kid here, you learn to compete with a fistful of Vaseline.

- Volleyball: Palming the ball is totally acceptable. That style was invented here, as there used to be palm trees by the courts.

- Softball: In the bottom half of the last inning, the home team can bat whichever hitters they want, in honor of nineteenth-century local baseball commissioner Judge Harry "Out of Order" Lemmish.

- Miniature Golf: On the course's eighteenth hole, the visitor has to play with a Super Ball.

- Horseshoes: Do whatever you want—nobody knows the rules to horseshoes.

- Basketball: Shots from behind the three-point line are worth four points, depending on how many minutes are left.

- Marco Polo: If you yell out "polio," you can punch "Marco" in the shoulder.

- Hockey: Offsides is only against the rules if it doesn't lead to a goal.

- Tennis: A ball on the line is "out." You don't like it, find someplace else to play, buddy.

- Soccer: You can touch the ball with your left hand. You didn't know that? You do now.

- Foosball: If you flick the ball off the table and into your opponent's face, that's two points.

- Fencing: Explain to your wounded opponent that everyone around here uses real swords.

UNDER
THE
CUE

With a pool cue resting across the width of a pool table, bet that you can roll a ball under the cue. The lip of the pool table isn't high enough, so when you demonstrate by rolling a ball, it keeps hitting the cue lying across. To win the bet, roll the ball under the table, and therefore under the cue. A cheap one, but hey, it works.

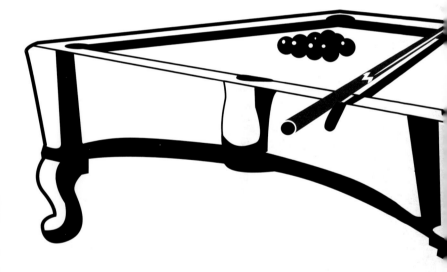

This is what I like to call a multipurpose scam. You can do it to lighten the mood and get a laugh out of the poor sucker that falls for it. Or you can really screw someone over, win back all the scratch you lost to him because you suck at pool, and make that person feel like a complete idiot. It is a lovely, versatile tool. —TR

ON THE NOSE

You're filling out the brackets for the basketball tournament, and your pal is boasting about the accuracy of his predictions for two years running. Well, if he wants to prove how on the nose he is . . .

WHAT IT'S GOOD FOR:
No matter how many points your buddy is ahead, for the entire two and a half weeks of the tourney, you can remind him what an idiot he looked like.

WHAT YOU NEED:
- A pencil
- A quarter
- A piece of paper

WHAT YOU DO:

1 Test his accuracy with a little challenge: Whoever can roll the quarter off his nose and get closest to the x wins.

2 First you will demonstrate how it's done. Flip over your brackets, placing the sheet of paper in front of you on the table. Draw an x right in the middle.

3 While looking straight ahead, place the quarter at the top of your forehead, edge facing out.

4 Now roll the quarter down until it reaches the tip of your nose and stop. Trying to guess where the x is below you, position your nose over it and let the quarter drop.

5 Take the pencil and draw a line around the quarter, making a circle where it landed on the paper. But make sure you apply a lot of pressure and circle the quarter a few times. This is key, as it will load the ridges of the quarter's edge with graphite from the pencil tip (see fig. 1).

6 Now when the mark attempts the same thing by rolling the quarter down his face, he will leave a dark line from his forehead to the tip of his nose without realizing it (see fig. 2). At this point, who really cares how close he gets to the x. Tell him he won. Tell him his accuracy is as good as he claims. This is one bet you won't mind losing.

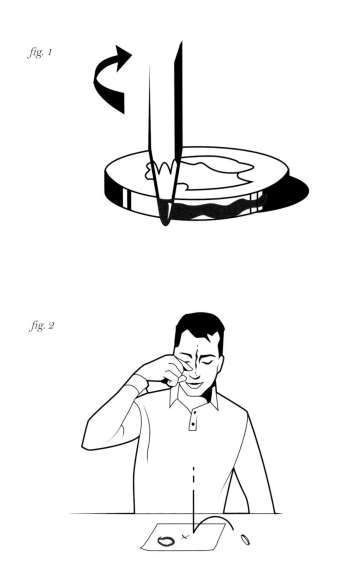

fig. 1

fig. 2

A HORSE RACING
HUNCH

There was an old grifter named Rummy Stewart. Like all grifters, Rummy loved playing hunches, and one night he had a dream that involved horses running in circles, and the number five kept coming to him. Over and over and over again. When he woke up, he couldn't help but realize it was May 5. Five-five on the calendar. He thought this was a good sign, so he went to the Hollywood Park racetracks outside of L.A. And while he was looking at the lineup of horses, he noticed in the fifth race was a horse—a horse named Cinco! Rummy was sure this was kismet. A sign. Meant to be. He went to the window to lay down a bet. Five dollars wouldn't be enough, but he wasn't able to put down five hundred. So he put down fifty-five dollars on the race.

The fifth race came, the horses flew out of the gate, down the track, and around the bend—and on that fifth day of the fifth month in the fifth race, the horse Cinco came in fifth.

TEAM PLAY

Most professional scammers would rather work solo, unless they are undertaking a Big Store con, then a full crew is needed to make the play. Working as a single-o allows the grifter to move about with ease, and you don't have to cut up the take with anyone else.

But you, my neophyte friend, might want to have some backup when you get your feet wet in the great ocean of con artistry. There is strength in numbers, and often you have to work as a team to be effective. But a con team is less like a football team with everyone running and jumping around and more like those guys that do that curling thing. You know, someone throws this round thing onto some ice, and then the others sweep to make sure it goes where it is supposed to go or something.

Sport playing is a perfect primer for working with a crew, since all team athletes know that practicing and diagram studying are wonderful, but game time brings its own necessary last-moment adjustments that need to be acted on immediately and with confidence. One of the keys to working as a crew is the use of the magic yes. Always agree with whatever lie your partner has put forth. This will add clarity to whatever concept is being sold and will make the round thing go where it is supposed to go on the ice.

Your team can do more than just support an untruth. They can also be a physical barrier between the mark and the rest of the world. Once you gain possession of the money, you are like a player with the ball. No matter how bad things get, your team's priority is your protection. They can gather around and isolate the victim so that no one can get to him and smarten up the chump. This is known as a freeze-out. It is always best to scam someone in an environment free from distractions such as logic and reason.

Another advantage to working with others comes into play if a hasty retreat is necessary. One of the crew can sneak out, start the car, and bring it around to the back door. When the moment comes, you can expedite your exit and safely watch that bunch of angry suckers in the rearview mirror growing smaller and smaller as you speed off to parts unknown. Score one for the visiting team.

THE RISE OF TITANIC

Even his name was a con: Legendary hustler Titanic Thompson was born Alvin Clarence Thomas in 1892. Though he was a very gifted athlete—especially at golf—Titanic's true calling was the proposition bet. Here is just a sample of his greatest sports cons:

1

Titanic challenged the world champ horseshoes player to a match for two thousand dollars. Unbeknownst to the champ, Thompson set up a forty-one-foot court, rather than the standard forty feet. Titanic had been practicing at the greater distance and easily won.

2

One of Titanic's standards was to play golf for money against someone wealthy, win, and then give the mark a chance to win his money back, double or nothing. And this time, Titanic would even switch to playing left-handed. Little did his marks know that Thompson was a natural lefty.

3

He also pulled the same ambidextrous scam when he played pool.

4

Titanic had a young African American golf hustler act as his caddy, so he could make the wager that even his caddy could beat his opponent of the day. (The young hustler was Lee Elder, who grew up to win many titles—legitimately—on the PGA tour and was the first African American to play in the Masters Tournament.)

5

Thompson made a thousand-dollar bet that he could drive a golf ball five hundred yards. Aware of his usual tricks, the men he bet against made Titanic swear this would take place at sea level, so that he would not simply hit the ball off the Grand Canyon. He then won by teeing off from the edge of Lake Erie . . . and watching the ball skid across its frozen February surface.

Another tactic of Titanic's was presetting a wager's outcome. Some examples include:

6

When he was six, he bet someone that he could throw a marked stone into a pond and his dog would retrieve it. He won the bet, as he had earlier loaded the pond bed with marked stones.

7

When traveling on a road he claimed to know rather well, Titanic would bet that a sign indicating the distance to the next town was off by five miles. The bet would be taken, the distance measured, and he would win. This was due to his having woken up early and moved the sign himself.

8

Titanic would bet that he could guess, within five, the number of watermelons on a truck. He'd make eight hundred dollars profit off the thousand-dollar bet, since he would have paid the driver earlier to give him the total count. Thompson would never "guess" the exact number, but was always close enough to win.

9

One time when this method didn't work was on a horse race in Tijuana. Titanic bet $150,000 on an eight-to-one long shot. He hedged his bets by paying off all the jockeys. If money wasn't enough incentive for the riders, he told them he had hired a sniper to pick off any horse (and jockey) that might cross the finish line before his choice. Unfortunately, Titanic's chosen horse fell and broke her leg down the stretch, leaving a field of nervous riders afraid to finish first.

NOT
BEFORE THE
BIG
GAME

It's the night before your interoffice softball championship game. You're out with your teammates and everyone is asking you to take it easy. You're the team star, after all. They don't want you getting too messed up before the big game. You tell them you'll be happy to forgo any drinking—but only if they can stop you.

Here's the bet you suggest: If they can keep you from drinking in a simple test, you'll pick up the tab for everyone and stay dry yourself. But if they can't, they have to not only let you have a couple of drinks, but pay for them too. You'll hold a pint of beer in your left hand, arm stretched out straight. The toughest guy can grab your forearm, anywhere from the wrist to the elbow, as hard as he wants. Hell, let two guys hold your wrist. That won't prevent you from getting that pint into your mouth. You have the strength of ten men when you're determined, right? How do you think you got the team to the finals in the first place?

When they take you up on it, reach over with your right hand and take the pint of beer out of your left hand and drink it.

TEES FOR TWO

You're reaching the end of the back nine, and it just hasn't been your day. Time to turn your luck around.

WHAT IT'S GOOD FOR:
Finally heading back to the clubhouse a winner.

WHAT YOU NEED:
- 2 golf tees

WHAT YOU DO:
1   Place a tee in each of the mark's hands, so he's holding them in the crook (or crotch) of his thumbs (see fig. 1).

2   Now challenge your mark to transfer the two tees to the opposite hands without dropping them or using anything other than his thumbs and index fingers.

3   When he gives up, show how it's done.

WHAT'S THE SECRET:
1   Place your left thumb on the bottom of the right-hand tee and your left index finger on the top (see fig. 2).

2   Then—careful, don't let go of the other tee—place your right thumb on the bottom of the left-hand tee and your right index finger on the top (see fig. 3).

3   Now twist your hands free, and you'll see the two tees have switched hands without getting tied up.

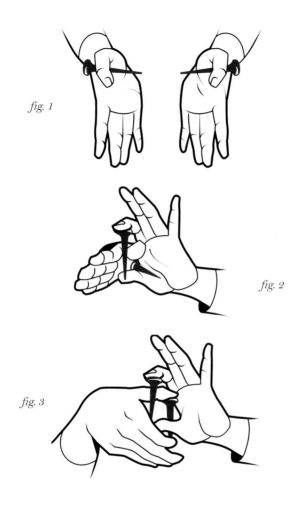

fig. 1

fig. 2

fig. 3

The key to this bit is to learn to do it smoothly. You don't have to do it fast to fool your mark. As a matter of fact, you don't want to do it fast. The slower you do it, the easier it looks and the deeper the hook will be sunk into the flesh of your victim. Doing a bit like this well is where the art *in the phrase* con artist *comes from. —TR*

THE GRIFTY FIFTY

Where there's sports, there's betting, and where there's betting, there's fire. So be warned, there's a three-alarm grift going around that aims to burn bad. Like the SCORE SCAM (see page 192), this deals with predicting the outcome of the game before it begins. But this one is so evil we include it here for you, the somehow-still-gullible ones, so you don't go chasing the sure thing this book is trying to show you doesn't exist.

The scam goes like this: The scammer picks a bunch of people he vaguely knows but who aren't close to each other—classmates, coworkers, old high school associates, friends of friends, and distant relatives—about fifty of them total. He e-mails them all friendly, personal e-mails that say, "Hey, I have a new buddy who is way deep into some heavy Vegas oddsmakers, and he's telling me they practically guaranteed the outcome of this week's game."

To twenty-five of the people he says that team A is going to win, and to the others he says team B will.

The next week he writes to the twenty-five to whom he sent the correct prediction. He tells twelve of them his insider is saying that in this week's matchup, team C is going to win, and he tells the other thirteen that team D will.

A week later, members of one of those groups think they're two for two. Not bad. He splits that winning group in half and does the same thing for the third week in a row. The game is played, and one of his predicted teams comes out with a win. Now, heading into the fourth week, there are at least six people who think they're on to something. And he does it again, and that means on the fifth week there are three people who are *convinced* they're four for four. This time, though, he calls each guy and says, "You won't believe it, but my insider is charging for the outcome of this week's game. You wanna go halfsies? Great. We'll each put in one hundred dollars." Thinking they're gonna be five for five, everyone agrees, and he just scammed his way to three hundred dollars doing nothing but sending some e-mails.

Here's the kicker: He only gives the same prediction to two of the three suckers. That ensures at least one guy—who has probably made a lot in the last few weeks—is going to pay even more for yet another pick. The grifter has at least one more week to score big before this con is over. And then he just finds another fifty . . .

SIX MEN OUT

Stuck in the dugout during a rain delay with the rest of the team? Get this scam going and you'll be hoping the sky never clears.

WHAT IT'S GOOD FOR:
A worthwhile reason for delaying your induction into the Hall of Fame for suspicion of gambling.

WHAT YOU NEED:
- 3 dice
- 6 suckers

WHAT YOU DO:

1 Have each of the six guys select a number between one and six so that they each have a different number assigned to them.

2 All the players put one dollar into the bank (you).

3 Now roll the three dice at once. Players win money if their number comes up in the following ways:

If a player's number is rolled on one of the dice, he doubles his money, making back his dollar plus one dollar from the bank.

If a player's number is rolled on two of the dice, he triples his money, making back his dollar plus an additional two dollars from the bank.

If a player's number is rolled on all three, he quadruples his money, making back his initial dollar plus three dollars from the bank.

Individual players might think their odds are pretty good—and feel free to encourage them to continue with the ol' gambling myth that the more they play, the more they stand to win. But the only favorable odds are yours. In fact, you will never lose anything, and if you're able to keep the game going, you'll come out quite ahead.

WHAT'S THE SECRET:
Since you've collected six dollars total before the dice are thrown . . .

If the roll of the dice turns up three different numbers, you pay two dollars to each of the three players, and your take is zero.

If two of the dice have the same number, you pay three dollars to one player and two dollars to the other, and you end up with one dollar.

If all three dice end up the same, you pay four dollars to one player and you pocket two dollars.

THE SCORE SCAM

You're in the concession stand line trying to get your beer and hot dogs before kickoff, and the guy in front of you is bragging about his perfect 50-yard-line seats. May as well make a wager to swap tickets with him. Tell him you're going to predict the score of the game before it even begins.

Now take out a pen and write down on a napkin: 0–0. Then show it to him. Because the score of the game before it begins is 0–0. It always is.

THE SUPER BET

You're at the game and the home team is losing. Again. And the guy next to you is saying there's no way they're making it to the Super Bowl. Tell him he might be right, so he can relax. In fact, you can make a prediction about the big game: You bet that the Super Bowl this year will be between San Diego and Tampa Bay. If he takes you up on it, point out that the Super Bowl will in fact be played between San Diego and Tampa Bay—that is, someplace in between.

THE TEN COMMANDMENTS

FOR CON MEN

Sports have rules, and the godfather of grift, Victor Lustig, thought flimflam should as well. So back in the 1940s, he came up with his Ten Commandments for Con Men. We have taken his gospel and revised it slightly for grifting in the new millennium.

1

Be a good listener. It's the listening, not the verbal razzmatazz, that will often endear the con man to his mark. If you've had a girlfriend who likes to describe her dreams, you've already mastered this one.

2

Similarly, no matter how many times you've told the same story, or how lame the small talk needs to be, never look bored.

3

Wait for the other person to reveal any political opinions, then agree with them—which is standard operating procedure for politicians, anyway.

4

Let the other person reveal religious views, then have the same ones. ("Oh, you also worship the Dark Lord by drinking virgin woodchuck blood? Me too!")

5

Hint at sex talk, but don't follow it up unless the other fellow shows a strong interest.

6

Try not to bring up sickness and disease.

7

Never pry into a person's personal life since they'll tell you
everything you need to know in due time. And if they don't,
that's when you hack into their e-mail.

8

There's no reason to brag. And this does include rapid fist-pumping.
Just let your importance be quietly obvious.

9

Never be untidy—but stop just short of "metrosexual."

10

Never get drunk. (Okay, nine out of ten ain't bad.)

I have never let my schooling interfere with my education.
—MARK TWAIN

CHAPTER 8

Ways to Scam at School

Institutes of higher learning are fertile grounds for marks to be truly schooled. Students, and especially professors, often think they're the next Einstein, and the smartest person can be the easiest to dupe. Besides, know-it-alls are so much more fun to fool. Set your sights on your fellow students, roommates, instructors, and drunks at frat parties. Class is in session . . .

CON-OPERATED WASHER

Dudes are scrounging for quarters and everything stinks—must be laundry day! So here's a dirty little way to get clean.

WHAT IT'S GOOD FOR:
Making a buddy pay to clean your underwear.

WHAT YOU NEED:
- 10 quarters
- 3 cups or glasses

WHAT YOU DO:
1 Bet your pal that he can't put the ten coins into the three glasses so that each glass contains an odd number of coins. (Come on, College Boy, you remember odd numbers: 1, 3, 5, 7, or 9.)

2 He won't be able to and might even claim it can't be done. On the contrary, our dirty-shirted amigo. Show him how by first placing three of the coins in one glass.

3 Then drop three coins in the next glass.

4 And, finally, drop four coins in the last glass.

5 Just when he's about to inform you that four isn't odd, you prove you're not done yet by taking one of the glasses with three coins and placing it *inside* the one with four.

6 Now there are technically seven coins inside the bottom glass, three in the top glass, and three in the untouched glass. How odd.

THE
FUTURE
STARTS
NOW

They say you make lifelong friends in college, and if you act quickly and wisely, you'll only be so lucky. For walking through campus as you read this are a bunch of eighteen-year-olds who you will desperately need at one point or another. Meet them, have lunch, invite them to parties, whatever it takes. Audit a class they're taking if that's going to give you an in. Mostly, act like you're a college recruiter wooing a star athlete. Because you *are* assembling a team, a team that will be playing for you.

In the world of grift, there have always been long cons and short cons, and the situation you now face is no different. Some of these guys will be mostly long cons, people to befriend now to help Future You. (He thanks you in advance, trust us.) Others are predominantly short cons, buddies to get you through the next four years. Yet they'll each have elements of both, which is why they should all be on your must-meet list starting today. The fate of the future—well, yours, anyway—depends on it.

THE BUSINESS STUDENT aka "The Gold Key"
This guy is mostly a long con, the exception being if he comes from money. In that case, there's the obvious advantage of getting in his inner circle—when Daddy visits, you'll be eating at the nicest steak house in town, and on spring break, you'll know no bounds. Otherwise, you'll just have to grin and bear it for the next few years. Deal with it. You know where Donald Trump's college buddies are hanging out every night? Nestled between a pair of women on a jet between New York and Paris. He's your future ticket into the world of truly wealthy suckers.

THE FACULTY MEMBER aka "The Inside Man"
He's mostly a short con, as the advantage is an ally with knowledge of, and access to, the inner sanctums of the administration. He'll be a great character witness with other professors if needed, and may even slip up with some great faculty gossip that can certainly come in handy. The long con is limited with this guy, although it's not a bad idea to have entrée to campus resources after graduation. And sure, you used to beat up the teacher's pet in elementary school and now you've become the thing you despised. That's life, friend, and it's time to come to terms with it.

THE COMPUTER SCIENCE MAJOR aka "The Dreamer"
Take a peek into a computer science class. Now locate the guy who seems the most laid-back. His shirt's untucked, he's smiling at some private thought, and mostly doodling instead of taking notes. He's your man. Yes, there's a chance he's going nowhere fast. But there's an equally good chance he's going to make $165 billion when he sells his I-had-insomnia-for-a-week-so-I-invented-this-thing Internet concept to Microsoft. When that happens, he's going to throw some wicked parties and, even more important, will always see his wealth as some sort of crazy fluke. This means he will be willing to fund his good friend's crazy-ass get-rich-quick ideas.

THE LAW STUDENT aka "The Protector"
You have no idea how many times in life you're going to need a good attorney—divorces, arrests, taxes, lawsuits, patents (for those crazy-ass get-rich-quick ideas)—but we can assure you this: You won't be able to afford a single one of them. In fact, as painfully boring as it might be, you'll probably want to buddy up with a couple of these guys. Good luck, and Godspeed.

(continued)

THE PREMED STUDENT aka "The Fixer"

Let's face it, you're gonna piss some people off. And there's a good chance at some point you're going to take a great fall. Therefore, you're going to need someone to put you back together again, Humpty. He's going to sew you up, give you pills, and make sure you make it to your next unfortunate encounter. That's why this new friend of yours is mostly a long con. But if there's an immediate gain to be made, it's probably that he has the inside scoop on any on-campus physical-experiments-for-cash opportunities, which certainly can't hurt. (If anything, they'll just feel like a bee sting.) The big bonus of being buddies with Mr. Premed is he's going to be so busy for the next hundred years that you're never really going to need to spend too much time with him at all. And that's the best kind of friend to have.

THE FINE ARTIST aka "The Mystery Man"

He's mostly a short con. Sure, he'll invite you to a lot of trippy parties and introduce you to some truly screwed-up (and fun) women. But the most important thing is he's creative and good with tools. He can silk-screen (great for phony "Security" T-shirts), make IDs, build props, and has access to everything—paint, welding supplies, wood, hardware, fabrics, etc.—to help with whatever your needs turn out to be. He also holds the Art Card, one of the major trump cards on campus, which allows you to do almost anything when you're together and pawn it off as "art." Park your car on the field if you can't find a spot—and he will say it's an installation piece. Get caught cheating and your buddy will announce it was really a performance that he's been planning. The real world doesn't give a crap about any of this, but in school, art doesn't have to play by the rules. Now neither do you.

THE DEFENSIVE BACK aka "The Muscle"

He's bigger than you are, but you make him laugh. That's good enough for him. And for you, it means he's got your back. That's all there is to it. Until Mr. Premed gets hooked up at a hospital or his own private practice, you need protection. The Defensive Back is a short con, but keep the friendship going as long as you can. If he ever goes pro, season tickets are always useful for buttering up a mark.

```
        1   2  3  4  5  6
 7  8   9 10 11 12 13
14 15  16 17 18 19 20
21 22 23 24 25 26 27
28 29 30 31
```

THE
BIRTHDAY
BET

When someone in your dorm building is having a floor party for her birthday, there's a good odds-in-your-favor bet to make that's perfectly themed. If there are over thirty people present, the odds are that two people there share the same birthday. Make the bet with someone and then go around the hall and have people call out their birthdays. Odds are you'll be right.

Best part is you can write up this experiment as an extra-credit essay for your statistics class.

This is not foolproof, but works enough of the time to make it worthwhile. And besides, the fact that there is a slight chance of failure should give you a bit of a thrill. Who wants to play it safe all the time? —TR

THE GRAND
SLAM

It looks like a drinking game. It feels like a bar bet. In reality, it's just a nasty little trick.

WHAT IT'S GOOD FOR:
Making a fool of that big dumb guy in your dorm or frat house.

WHAT YOU NEED:
- A glass of water
- A penny
- A napkin
- A flat surface

WHAT YOU DO:

1 This can be done with just one other person—your mark. But having an extra person or two improves the payoff. Suggest a contest in which the person who can get the penny to land on the napkin wins. The catch: The penny must drop from your forehead.

2 Demonstrate for the assembled group: Place the napkin on the edge of the table. Wet the penny in the glass of water and stick it to your forehead. (Really dumb guys will already be impressed.) While leaning over the edge of the table, gently tap the back of your head a few times until the penny drops. It doesn't matter where it lands.

3 Someone else wants to give it a try? You're in charge: You wet the penny; you stick it to his forehead. Again, it makes no difference whatsoever where the coin lands.

4 Eventually your mark will want a shot. Dumb guys always want to try. This time, behind the mark's back, take the penny out of your hand. With your wet fingers, stick nothing to the mark's forehead. Just press your damp thumb right in there. He won't know the difference.

5 The mark will slap the back of his head. Nothing happens. "Try again," you encourage. Nothing. "Ooh, close. Try again." Nothing. He'll begin hitting himself harder. "Again. Another shot. It's about to fall." He'll probably whack himself even harder, in a last attempt to dislodge the coin.

6 Depending on how dumb he is, he'll figure it out sooner or later. And maybe you'll get a slap on the head as payback. But it's well worth it, for making a moron look like a fool.

There is no money to be won with this bit, but it will feel good to do this. And as has been put forth earlier, pleasure is what it is all about. —TR

OLD SCHOOL'S IN SESSION

History class boring you with the industrial revolution or that Renaissance nonsense again? Let's cover something more interesting: a classic golden age grift from days gone by.

Nowadays, a little lighthearted trickery at a train station is liable to bring you face-to-face with automatic-weapon-toting guards, attack dogs, and a spot on Homeland Security's most-wanted list. But train stations used to be favorite locales of the golden age con man.

The con is on the lookout for a lone traveler who is changing trains, with some time to kill at the gate. Once he's found his mark, the con man tells him that he is getting on that same train and suggests going to a nearby bar. Outside the bar, they happen upon the accomplice, who is faking an absurd Southern accent. After a request for directions is denied, the accomplice accuses these two Northerners of being rude and cheap. The con man protests. "And we will buy you a drink to prove it!" he says. The accomplice refuses. "Okay, we'll buy you a cigar!"

"Forget it," says the accomplice.

"Hey, pal, we're just trying to be nice," says the con man. "If you won't accept a free drink, let's match for it." (To "match" coins is basically a variation on rock, paper, scissors, in which you reveal heads or tails. With three people, the odd man out wins.) So the con man whispers conspiratorially to the mark, "You show heads each time,

I'll show tails, and he'll lose every time." No matter what the accomplice reveals, he'll match with one of the two.

First match, the con man wins. The accomplice ups the ante but keeps it small. Maybe five bucks. This time, the mark wins. Oooh, this is getting fun. "Not very good at this, are you, you dumb Southerner!" taunts the con man. Now that Southerner is mad! The con man says, "Okay, put your money where your big Southern mouth is. Let's play for all the money we've got on us." The con man gives a little wink to the mark: *We're still in this together.* And in this match, the con man wins. Shocking! The accomplice hands over all his money, as does the mark. The accomplice storms off in disgust.

The con man starts splitting up the total "winnings" with the mark. Just then the accomplice reappears. "Aha! I knew you two Northerners were in cahoots! You tried to con me."

"No, no," begs the con man, "we've never met!" The mark sincerely agrees.

"Okay, prove it," says the accomplice. "You walk that way and you walk that way."

The con man whispers to the mark, "Don't worry, we'll meet on the train—in the café car." The con man walks off with all the money. And the now-penniless mark boards the train and never sees him again. Not even one penny to match with someone else. That is old-school cold.

KNOT
A SMOKER

It's that one night of the entire semester when you've decided to hit the books, but there's that jerk who won't shut up and keeps blowing smoke in your face. Make him the following wager, and if you win, he has to close his yap and put out his smokes.

WHAT IT'S GOOD FOR:

Honestly, at the end of the day it's not good for anything. Party Guy always trumps Study Guy. See Darwin's theory of evolution.

WHAT YOU NEED:

• A cigarette pack
• A cigarette

WHAT YOU DO:

1 Bet that you can tie a cigarette into a knot.

2 Once the bet is taken, remove the cellophane wrapping from the pack and lay it down flat on the table.

3 Place the cigarette at one end of the cellophane and roll it up so that the cellophane completely and tightly wraps the cigarette. The cellophane should be longer than the cigarette and thus stick out further on both sides (see fig. 1).

fig. 1

4 With the wrapping now tightly holding the cigarette together, you will be able to use the cellophane to tie a knot, therefore doing the same to the cigarette.

5 If the jerk persists—and he will, that's what jerks do—next pull A HANDFUL (see page 124).

I like this scam because it takes advantage of the beleaguered smoker, who has enough trouble these days finding a place where smoking is allowed. If you can't kick someone who is down, then when can you kick them? —TR

THE **NEW YOU**

It's freshman orientation, so *please* take a few minutes to reinvent yourself before it's too late and you're still just the guy who shit his pants in French class two years ago. And since no one here knows that was you, let's just say it wasn't. You didn't even *take* French in high school. See how easy that was? There truly is no better time in life to create a new you than your time in college.

THE NEW NAME
Your middle name is the quickest solution, and actually legal. So start using it when meeting people, signing papers, and dealing with the administration. This will often create minor confusion that can always be played in your favor. You're one person when you need to be, the other when you don't (although they're always getting confused with each other!). It will also help separate you from your past (on the off chance someone Googles "shit his pants" and "French class").

THE NEW PAST
Remember when your friend came back from a summer in New York and said he and a buddy got drunk, stole a rowboat at midnight with two chicks, and, after being swept out to sea, had to get rescued by a helicopter? Good, because that now happened to you. In fact, all his crazy adventures are now yours. After all, you listened to those stories so often you can recite them by heart. So start reciting, because you never know how people will react. ("Wow, you've had a pretty amazing life so far! Want to have sex?")

THE NEW LOOK

Clothes say so much about us, so now's the time to come up with a whole new vocabulary. Remember when your pal bought a seersucker suit for the spring dance that actually looked pretty great—and everyone told him so? And remember how you wished you'd thought of that?

THE NEW COOL

You're suddenly as cool as all the coolest kids back at home, combined. Literally. Because you're stealing their greatest hits. The unknown bands and obscure movies they introduced you to—you can now pay it all forward as your discoveries.

THE NEW WAY OUT

Don't feel like helping your roommate carry in boxes? "My lung collapsed this summer, and I'm supposed to hold off on that sort of thing for a few months." Hook up with a girl during the first week but don't want to keep things going? "Sorry, my parents are splitting up and it's really confusing me." The best kinds of personal tragedies, family issues, and medical problems are the made-up ones. Be creative to get what you want and avoid what you don't.

THE NEW OUTLOOK

All the observations your brainy high school pal used to make ("You know you're getting older when everyone keeps telling you how young you are . . .") are now yours. Finally, you too can be astute and profound.

THE NEW HUMOR

What about that guy in homeroom who used to say all those hilarious things before the bell? What guy? That was you! Prove it by using his jokes and sarcastic cracks.

DOUBT

I'm not sure that the following idea I am about to describe will make sense, but let's see if it does.

The preceding sentence makes you want to read the rest of this, don't it? And the reason you are intrigued is because there was an element of doubt in it. If I had started with "I am going to put forth something important that will be good for you," you probably would still have read the rest of this, but while you did so, you would also be thinking, "I'll be the judge of that."

Doubt is a truly wonderful tool. No one wants to hang around with a know-it-all, and no one's going to take up a too-good-to-be-true betcha from a guy that already seems sure of the outcome.

It ain't an effective approach to just tap a guy on the shoulder and say, "I bet I can shove the entire handle of this spoon up my nose." He will gaze at you the way a pig looks at a wristwatch and then walk away.

No, the scam scenario should go more like this: You're eating your soup at the counter, chatting a little about the weather with the fellow next to you—but all the while you're looking at your spoon, quietly laughing to yourself and sort of shaking your head. Eventually, you mention in passing, "You know, I knew a guy in college once who could fit the entire handle of a spoon in his nose. It was the damndest thing I ever saw." You can even shake your head a bit more, still in disbelief after all these years.

Then move on. More talk about whether or not it's gonna rain this weekend, before looking back at the spoon. "I wonder how far it would go . . . if I could do it. If I tried."

He shrugs. "Probably not far. Look at that thing."

"I know, I know. But I saw him do it. It can't be *impossible* or anything . . ."

Even as you inch closer to making the bet, you're never losing some sense of doubt that you can't help but shake. Because your doubt will only make his doubt grow to the point of practically announcing that *it just can't be done.*

And that's when you make the bet.

Even after you win, don't let that doubt fully disappear, because your disbelief is the key at this stage. Even though you came out victorious, appear just as surprised as anyone that it worked. "Holy shine-ola, I can't believe that worked!" Laugh it off, almost as if the winning was a fluke. And maybe it was a fluke. Keep up that angle and you might be able to rope him in for another one.

The true master of the use of doubt was George DeVol, the nineteenth-century king of the Mississippi riverboat three-card monte. George would be sitting around the boat's lounge after dinner, smoking a cigar with the boys, when he would say, "You know, I recently lost a bundle to a fellow who played a little game with three cards. I kept those cards—I have them here somewhere. Oh, here they are. I think the guy was doing something like this . . ." He would then proceed to throw the monte in a way that looked like he didn't know what he was doing. When the suckers lost, and they always did, it felt to them that *they* had done something wrong, not good old George. DeVol made a fortune this way.

I guess what I am trying to say is (there's that doubt again) that doubt is a wonderful tool, so use it to your advantage, my young friend.

The less you seem to know, the more they'll think they do. Which is perfect since in reality they don't know a damn thing . . . I think.

THE
**WIPE
-OUT**

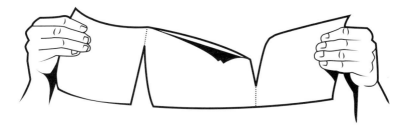

It's the last roll of toilet paper already? How many assholes live here? Before you resort to using Kleenex or the campus newspaper, make a bet with your roomie. Loser goes to buy more TP. In advance, rip off four three-square sections. You've got two perforated tears on each, right? Rip one of those from top to bottom, leaving about a half inch unripped. Rip the other one bottom to top, also leaving a half inch unripped. Do this for each three-square section.

Now, bet your roomie that he can't hold one of the end squares in each hand, and with one pull, end up with three separate squares. Let him try a couple of times. It can't be done. Or can it? Tell your roomie that you're such a good sport, he doesn't have to buy more unless you can do it. Take one square in each hand and, before pulling, grip the middle square with your lips. The squares will pull apart easily, and you win. Just make sure it's unused TP before you put it in your mouth.

THREE-CUP MONTE

You just woke up in the frat house living room, underneath a pile of trash and other first-year pledges. The place is a mess that you're going to have to take care of right away. But there's good news. Besides the fact that it seems like no one stuck a candle in your butt as a "practical joke," there are a hell of a lot of empty red plastic cups lying around. Time to clean up, if you know what we mean.

WHAT IT'S GOOD FOR:
Winning some beer money, of course.

WHAT YOU NEED:
• 3 empty, identical cups

WHAT YOU DO:

1 Line up the three cups, upside down.

2 Tell the nearest stooge that when you turn around, he should put a bottle cap under one of the cups and leave that cup right where it is.

3 Next he's going to take the other two cups and switch their positions.

4 When he's done with that, you turn around and correctly reveal where the bottle cap is hidden.

WHAT'S THE SECRET:
The cups can't really be totally identical. While they should seem that way, make sure when you're gathering the three cups to pick one that has some minor difference that only you can notice. (Or make a mark yourself. This is the precise reason that humans have fingernails.) Perhaps a small nick near the lip or a small scratch along the side or a very subtle dent. This is the one you will be paying attention to. If this marked cup is in the same position when the mark is done, that means the cap is under it, since the two *other* cups swapped places. If it has moved, the cup with the cap is (a) not the marked cup and (b) not the one in the marked cup's original position (because the marked cup changed positions with the other noncap cup).

STUDY BREAK

Damn the no. 2 pencil, the harbinger of serious life-deciding exams that never seem to end. Take out your frustration during your next study group session with the following wager. Pick an innocent bystander to hold a pencil tight and horizontal with both hands. Now take a dollar, fold it the long way, and bet your mark that he can't whip the bill down hard enough to snap the pencil in half. Not only that, but bet that once he fails, you will be able to do it.

Let the mark go first, and give him three tries. After he pathetically strikes the pencil without effect for the third time, take the dollar from him. Feel free to try twice and fail, to give the evening a sense of false drama, and then for your third attempt, raise the dollar and bring it down hard—breaking the pencil right in half! All you have to do is make sure your index finger comes out at the last moment, hidden behind the bill, and then comes back right after the snap.

Also make sure you're hitting the pencil with your knuckle, or the pencil won't be the thing making the loudest snap. —TR

THE TEN-SPOT TRICK

On the first day of American History 101, ask the chump in front of you if he's got a ten-dollar bill. If so, bet the money that he can't name the president on the front of it. Alexander Hamilton? Even if he happens to guess the man's name, he's wrong. Hamilton was never president, just secretary of the Treasury.

Now, if you happen to be studying for this class in the cafeteria and pull this scam over a snack break, there's an additional thing you can do, which we like to call . . .

NOW LOOK LEFT, MR. HAMILTON

Hamilton is looking to his right in his portrait on the ten. Just bet that you can make him look from right to left. You won't fold the bill or turn it upside down or anything, and you won't use a mirror. You're just going to sit at the table and hold it like you're doing, and he will just suddenly look the other way. When you're taken up on it, hold the ten spot behind a clear glass of water. Looking through the glass, you'll see ol' Alex facing to the right. Now slowly move the ten away from the glass, and once his picture moves a few inches away, Alexander Hamilton's head will suddenly flip to look the opposite way. Just one in a long, long line of two-faced politicians.

I believe that you should always *add insult to injury, and this one-two punch works well toward this end. Hopefully you won the mark's ten with the second bit and quickly got that winning money into your pocket. But if the mark beefs, give him a chance to win it back. Bring the wadded-up ten out of your pocket and play a game of "guess which hand the ten is in." Hold the ten in your right hand. Put both hands together as if you were praying with the money between them. Separate your hands into two fists with the bill in one of them. Make it obvious which hand holds the bill. Let your mark guess by asking, "Where is the ten?" The sucker will guess, and you will open your hand and show that the bill is there—but when you unfold the bill, it is a one-dollar bill, not the ten. The mark lost and you keep the ten. The trick is to keep a wadded-up one-dollar bill in your pocket at all times in case this scenario should arise and you can take advantage of it. When it happens, you switch bills when you put the crumpled-up ten in your pocket. Yes, it is a bit nutty to walk around with a bill crumpled up in your pocket, but it is worth ten bucks each time you work this scam. —TR*

FLIMFLAM
FINAL EXAM

Okay, students of scammery: We've almost reached the end of your formal studies. (But do understand that being a Modern Conman involves a lifetime of learning, adjusting to new scenarios, trends, technology, and purchasing future Modern Conman products.) Before we offer you congratulations on your con graduation, you will need to take this test. It will review how well you've absorbed the crucial information in this bible of bamboozlement, while testing your overall preparedness for this new life you've chosen. So get out your no. 2 pencils. The ones you haven't snapped in half in the STUDY BREAK scam (see page 218), that is.

1   To win at NIM, you and your mark's matches on each turn must add up to
   (a) 17
   (b) 4
   (c) 3
   (d) Irrelevant; set the matches ablaze and down your mark's drink while he is running away like a scared little girl.

2   In con artist circles, *geetus* is a synonym for
   (a) alcohol
   (b) a mark
   (c) money
   (d) your inbred cousin from the Deep South

3 Con artists need to keep excellent track of time, regardless of whether they've been banned from a bar for ninety-nine days, instructed to stay out of South Carolina altogether for eighteen months, or are waiting for a fake license to expire. Along these lines, how many months have thirty days? _____

4 In a crew of con men, the "innocent bystander" who sides with the person pulling the con is known as
(a) the stick
(b) the wall man
(c) the steerer
(d) the guy who can least afford another conviction

5 Joseph "Yellow Kid" Weil gained fame by
(a) perfecting the Big Store scam
(b) working medicine shows selling rainwater
(c) coining the phrase *confidence man*
(d) causing an outbreak of yellow fever throughout the Northwest

6 A modern con man must stay up-to-date on all changes in currency, as the weight and texture of a coin can greatly affect the outcome of a dexterity-based scam. World War II required copper to be used for ammunition, causing pennies issued in 1943 to be made of steel. But why are 1941 pennies worth more than 1940 pennies?

_____

_____

7 If a con goes bad, Todd Robbins suggests
(a) climbing out the bathroom window
(b) kicking your mark in the groin
(c) both of the above
(d) Todd Robbins? Who's that? Name sounds vaguely familiar, but it's certainly not an individual involved in any sort of wagers involving deception.

(continued)

8 Cheyenne, Wyoming, was the stomping grounds of the dollar-store con artist
(a) Ben Marks
(b) Soapy Smith
(c) Lou Blonger
(d) Why did you guess Todd Robbins again? You are obsessed with that guy. What are you, in love with him? Forget you ever heard the name, if you know what's good for you!

9 We cannot stress enough the importance of precisely timing your escape and double-checking the route—even if you're pulling a con on a boat. Say a rope ladder is hanging over the side, with the end touching the water. The rungs are two feet apart, and the tide is rising at a rate of four inches per hour. At the end of six hours, how many rungs will be underwater? _____

10 When pulling the coin-flipping prediction con, the code your date needs to follow is
(a) heads, say something; tails, say nothing
(b) heads, say nothing; tails, say something
(c) alternate between a and b
(d) don't grab the coin and run off to go shoe shopping

ANSWERS:

1 b

2 c

3 Eleven of the months have thirty days in them, moron.

4 a

5 b

6 Because $19.41 is more than $19.40 by one cent (whoops, sorry, our proof-reader forgot the commas in 1941 and 1940).

7 c

8 a

9 None; the boat will also rise with the tide.

10 c

HOW YOU DID:

9 or 10 correct: You've joined the ranks of the few, the proud . . . the Modern Conmen.

7 or 8 correct: Begin with the basic scams and work your way up—you're almost there.

5 or 6 correct: Leave this book in your bathroom and review it a few more times before attempting any cons. Hopefully a few bouts of food poisoning will force the study time you need to properly prepare yourself.

4 or less correct: You like bright colors, yes? Hooray! Bright colors good! You happy boy! Almost time for snacks!

IN CONCLUSION
"BLOW OFF"

I find a tear in my eye and sadness in my heart as I realize that we are coming to the end of our little tutorial on how to do wrong the right way.

Yes, I do feel a sense of accomplishment and pride about all the brilliant material we have laid out for you in these pages. It is a bountiful banquet of bunco that we have served up unto you. I chuckle as I conjure up the thought that you are now compiling a list of all the people that will be victims of the lovely malevolence that you now have at your disposal.

But at the same time, I feel blue that I must bring this tome to a close and part company with you. You have learned so much, and yet there is so very much more to be said about the art of doing harm to others.

Still, this book is a good start. So take what is here and make bad use of this information. Don't put it off. Do unto others before they do unto you. If you haven't pulled your first scam yet, do it soon. Do it today. Taste the sweetness of success and you will be hooked. So get out there and bat away.

And as you are conning your way into the hearts and wallets of others, I will be there standing in the shadows watching you . . . and smiling.

—Todd Robbins

ACKNOWLEDGMENTS

One last thing before we disappear around the corner.
Colin Dickerman, Miles Doyle, George Griffith,
Rob Hickman, Kate Lee, and Jordan Roter . . . *thank you.*

A NOTE ON THE AUTHORS

Todd Robbins is a New York–based entertainer who has appeared on *The Tonight Show with Jay Leno*, *The Late Show with David Letterman*, *Late Night with Conan O'Brien*, and *Good Morning America*. He stars in the DVD series the Modern Conman Collection.

The Modern Conman Collective consists of Gadi Harel and Marcel Sarmiento, proprietors of the Los Angeles–based production company Hollywoodmade and creators of the Modern Conman Collection DVD series, and Jack Silbert, a magazine editor and humor writer.